The Solution Focused Way

Incorporating Solution Focused Therapy Tools and Techniques into Your Everyday Work

Simon Proudlock

The Solution Focused Way

Incorporating Solution Focused Therapy Tools and Techniques into Your Everyday Work

Simon Proudlock

Routledge
Taylor & Francis Group
LONDON AND NEW YORK

First published 2011 by Speechmark Publishing Ltd.

2 Park Square, Milton Park, Abingdon, Oxfordshire OX14 4RN
52 Vanderbilt Avenue, New York, NY 10017

Routledge is an imprint of the Taylor & Francis Group, an informa business

First issued in paperback 2018

British Library Cataloguing in Publication Data
A catalogue record for this book is available from the British Library.

ISBN 978-1-138-41477-8 (pbk)
ISBN 978-0-86388-753-6 (pbk)

To Dr Esmaeil Mahdavi – Your wise words guide me with every client.
And to my dad, Michael, who helped me find many solutions.

Contents

Foreword

Almost a quarter of a century has passed since the late Steve De Shazer and Insoo Kim Berg's first publications about Solution Focused Therapy (SFT). In that quarter century, solution focused approaches have been widely applied and taken up in business, education, criminal justice, counselling and mental health settings. Curiously, and possibly because of the very simplicity and brevity of the solution focused approach, SFT has never really captured the attention of major psychological and psychotherapy research groups in the same way as much more complex approaches such as Cognitive Behaviour Therapy (CBT). Reflecting this, several years ago I gave a series of lectures titled 'Solution Focused Brief Therapy, Always the Bridesmaid Never the Bride?' which described my own very limited work in this field. Despite this, a sizeable body of literature has grown up which demonstrates that solution focused approaches can be used in a huge range of settings, to help individuals, couples, groups, companies and organisations identify and enact solutions to a vast range of different problems.

The solution focused approach has many attractions. In a cash-strapped world, it is hard to ignore an approach which holds the potential to help individuals, couples and organisations find solutions to painful or seemingly intractable problems and to do this in a rapid fashion, through the application of simple techniques and in ways which are sparing of limited resources. My own studies and those of others who have worked in the field demonstrate another attraction of SFT, which is that the simplicity of the approach with its common-sense underlying assumptions means that people with no prior knowledge of SFT can rapidly pick up the key techniques and learn to apply them in their day-to-day practice. The diversity of the SFT literature demonstrates that the approaches and techniques which Simon Proudlock has so ably described in this volume can also be readily integrated with a huge and diverse range of professional, therapeutic and educational ideologies and approaches.

In my own field, which is that of mental health, the last five to ten years have seen the rise of the recovery movement and the adoption of recovery principles as official UK mental health policy. The recovery movement rejects psychiatric labels, patient status and an exclusive clinical focus on problems in favour of a new emphasis on strengths, citizenship, quality of life and collaboration. This has created a fertile ground for the further incorporation of solution focused approaches into everyday practice. In the new world into which we are moving, it seems likely that the role of the mental health practitioner will increasingly be that of coach rather than expert. Perhaps finally, after a quarter of a century in which SFT has always been the bridesmaid and never the bride, the time of the respectful solution focused practitioner has finally come!

Two decades have passed since I first encountered SFT and began to experiment with incorporating solution focused approaches into my own practice. Looking back, I think that my own journey would have been easier if I had had access at the start to a comprehensive, accessible and well-written text such as this. The techniques and approaches described here are grounded in practice and, indeed, it has been my privilege to witness and supervise Simon's creative use of these approaches with a varied range of clients, in individual, couple and group settings. In my own work I have found that after being introduced to solution focused approaches, clinicians often begin to cautiously experiment with them and gradually gain confidence in their use, coming to use these techniques more and more as their confidence grows.

Although written in a very accessible style, this book incorporates a wealth of resources which I am sure will be of value to solution focused practitioners of all levels of experience pretty much regardless of the client groups they work with. Finally then, success breeds success, so I commend this book to the reader and suggest that you read it, think about it and then get out there and begin to use the approaches Simon has described and discover for yourself the power and utility of focusing on solutions.

Professor Nigel Wellman, Independent Research & Training Consultant,
Wellman Research & Consulting
Associate Professor of Health & Human Science,
Thames Valley University, England 2011

Acknowledgements

I've been privileged to have many great teachers throughout my career. These teachers have come in many different forms: from the formal teachers such as lecturers, supervisors, colleagues and trainers to the informal ones such as clients, friends and family, authors, writers of song lyrics, movies and television and partners – basically anyone or anything that feeds my development as a psychologist, and more recently as a trainer and author.

Over time these teachers have given me a wealth of ideas and concepts that I have assimilated into my work, either in their entirety, or as a foundation for an exercise or task I could use with a client. A training course on 'Cognitive Behaviour Therapy for Anxiety' could ignite a solution focused exercise on relationships.

As a result of all of these influences on my work, when I came to write this book I was brimming with ideas from my practice that I have now developed into more formal exercises and pages for this book. Unfortunately I am left with a vacuum when it comes to acknowledging some of the source of my inspiration. Wherever possible I have done so, but if I have omitted to acknowledge any of my 'teachers', please accept my apologies.

On a more practical production front, I would like to thank Caroline Stone for reviewing the many exercises included in the book, Dr Trevor Powell for introducing me to Speechmark and for his encouragement to write the book, and Professor Nigel Wellman for his continued support.

And finally my wife Eve – my sounding board, spelling and grammar checker, first-line copy editor and protector of the English language. Try as I might, I just couldn't get the Americanisms past her! Thank you for 'utilizing' your skills and 'summarizing' the errors of my ways!

Preface

This book came about a little by accident. A very forward thinking manager of the Crisis team in the Wokingham Community Mental Health Team asked me to put together a training programme for her staff which would allow them to utilise the tools and techniques of Solution Focused Therapy (SFT). After delivering the training I discussed it with my supervisor, Dr Trevor Powell, who encouraged me to put together a book proposal for Speechmark. They liked it. And the rest is history.

After the initial jubilations had calmed down I was hit with the daunting realisation – 'I actually have to write this thing!' So over the last year I have immersed myself in everything solution focused. I have formalised the many solution finding tools I have been using over the past few years, converted song lyrics into solution finding exercises and presented what I think is useful about Solution Focused Therapy. I hope you like it.

The structure of the book is aimed at giving someone new to SFT the chance to really get to grips with the concepts and applications. The first two chapters look at the basic tenets of SFT and how effective it can be. There is ample evidence highlighting how effective SFT is with a variety of populations. What I've done is to offer you a snapshot of the variety of its applications and efficacy.

The next two chapters look at how change happens and the effect that the therapeutic relationship has on this psychological change. Sometimes I feel I'm in the 'change business', and as a result I felt I needed to dedicate some space to see how this change happens – what are the key elements that facilitate change in our clients?

Chapter 5 (From problems to solutions: changing the focus of the practitioner) encourages the practitioner to start to see the client in a different way. Packed full of exercises to help this shift, the section ends with common barriers to use and how to overcome them.

Armed with the key elements, basic assumptions and central philosophy of SFT, and a new understanding of the client, we move on to the most important part of our work – building solutions. In this chapter we start to look at the integral components of SFT – non-problem talk, the stance of not knowing, compliments, goal setting, the Miracle Question, exceptions and scaling. We end the chapter by briefly examining breaks and feedback in SFT and how useful they can be in the practical applications of your work.

Chapter 7 (Speciality applications) presents four different areas in which SFT has proved to be effective. I chose to write sections on crisis management, relationships, anger and alcohol simply because these are the issues I am faced with on a consistent basis. SFT can be used with a whole host of populations and presenting problems and, as can be seen from this chapter, the approach for each is very much the same. All that is required is to fine-tune the skills presented in the Building solutions section (Chapter 6).

The biggest chapter of the book, Chapter 8, offers you the chance to start using some of the exercises I have been using over the last few years, together with some new ones developed for this book. Generally there is no hard and fast rule as to when to use a given exercise – that choice is left to you as the practitioner. If you have a client who is fascinated with movies, try using 'My life as a movie'. Likewise, if you feel your client is struggling to know what they want in a relationship, try 'Relationship shopping' with them. The choice of exercises is dependent on what you know about the client and your relationship with them.

Solutions are not just for therapy

A large part of this book references the 'therapy session', 'the therapist' and 'the client'. This is really for ease of description of how the themes in this book work, but the techniques described relate to so much more than a therapy session. SFT is used in education, business, social work, within inpatient care, with pain management and with families. I am fully aware that some outstanding work goes on outside a therapy session. This book simply aims to get you thinking about the people you work with in a different way. In order to reinforce this, wherever possible I have used 'practitioner' to refer to you, the professional, trying to facilitate and support change with the individuals you work with.

There may also be references to Solution Focused Brief Therapy – SFBT. This is the full name of Solution Focused Therapy, but in much of the literature the two terms are used interchangeably. My preference in this book has been to use Solution Focused Therapy – SFT.

A little about me ...

It was never my intention to enter the world of psychological therapy. My BSc was in Economics and Computer Science with the intention of working in commerce or IT. But three years of computer science was enough. Fortunately, my dissertation was on human–computer interaction, bringing me into contact with Psychology.

Many counselling courses later, and a move to Massachusetts, USA for nearly five years, led me to completing my MSc in Mental Health Counselling. This allowed me to experience SFT first hand, from the country that invented it and that utilises it the most. Not content with being a fully trained therapist, I took a week off my job and trained to be a cocktail bartender – one of the best uses of my annual leave. Mojito anyone?

Currently I work in adult mental health as a Chartered Counselling Psychologist. A very innovative Clinical Director has allowed me to incorporate the use of SFT into my practice within the National Health Service (NHS) and has encouraged me to facilitate more groups where solutions are the focus. I remain constantly surprised at how effective SFT is in my work; always amazed at the great solutions clients can find. I hope you can start to see something similar.

Introduction

> **'Problems can become opportunities when the right people come together.'**
> *Robert Redford*

We're surrounded by solutions. You only have to look in the *Yellow Pages* to find a whole host of companies offering you solutions to all of your everyday problems. Accounting solutions, plumbing solutions, IT solutions – it seems to be a great way to market your business.

Although this book is about Solution Focused Therapy (SFT), it doesn't really offer you any solutions to give to the people you work with. Instead it allows you to work with your clients to help them design and implement their own solutions. The solution focused techniques in this book are designed to complement and enhance your already competent skills as a practitioner in your field. I'm not looking to re-invent the wheel (I've been told there's little market for it in today's climate), but simply to give you another set of tools.

Without a formal theory or model, when using SFT we are able to be fully attentive to what the client is saying instead of attempting to try to 'fit' someone into the theory or model we are working with. Cognitive Behaviour Therapy looks for thinking distortions; Schema Focused Therapy looks for early maladaptive schemas; Psychodynamic Therapy looks for transference and countertransference. Listening to the client in this way could mean that we are missing out on the solutions that the client has within them.

Anyone can go into the room and ask the Miracle Questions, scaling questions or questions looking for exceptions – some of the basic tenets of SFT. But what I hope to impart in this book are the reasons why we ask those questions. What answers are we looking for? But more importantly, what's the bigger picture we are trying to help the client draw with these answers?

And once we have the answers, what next? These questions are simply guiding our curiosity; searching for the solutions, resources and resilience that we know are hiding somewhere within our client. The client is navigating us to their solution; we as therapists are simply the drivers, knowing when to put the foot on the pedal to move the conversation forward, and when to put our foot on the brake to amplify the gem of information the client has just given us.

What about the problem?

A common misperception of SFT is that it ignores the problem. We would struggle to form any type of therapeutic relationship with the client if we ignored the very essence of what brings them to therapy. Being solution focused doesn't mean we have to ignore the problem; it just means that we focus our attention and energies on discovering how the client would see their life if the problem disappeared. By taking this strengths-based positive approach, we strengthen our relationship with the client and empower them to tackle not only their current problem but problems that may occur in the future. This difference between a problem focused approach and a solution focused approach is innovatively described by Bannink:

Suppose you are hungry and decide to eat in a restaurant. After having waited for some time, you are invited to take a seat and the manager introduces himself. He asks you questions regarding your hunger: 'How hungry are you? For how long have you been preoccupied with this feeling? Were you hungry in the past? What role did hunger play at home with your family or with other relatives? What disadvantages and possible advantages does hunger have for you?' After this, having become even hungrier, you ask if you can now eat. But in addition the manager wants you to complete some questionnaires about hunger (and perhaps about other issues that the manager finds important). Once everything is finished, a meal is served to you that you did not order, but that the manager claims is good for you and has helped other hungry people. What are the chances of you leaving the restaurant feeling satisfied?

(Bannink, 2007, p87)

Driving and Solution Focused Therapy

Therapy in general could be likened to driving. All competent drivers regularly use their rear view mirror to see what might be coming up from behind that may affect their way forward.

All good drivers know that focusing too much on what's behind them is not beneficial to their driving – they will miss out on the dangers and hazards of what is coming up right in front of them. True Solution Focused Therapy builds on this idea – looking behind us at what has happened in our lives hinders us from concentrating on the here and now, and blinkers us from looking into the future, at what's ahead.

But at times, as when driving, it can be irresponsible to not look in our rear-view mirror. By not doing so, by not checking what may be behind us, we may cause a hazard to others and ourselves. Therapy can be the same. At times, we need to check back to what's behind us, our past, to see if it may be hindering what we are doing right now and affecting us attaining our goals for the future.

Solution Focused Therapy is a great tool to use to help us keep the focus for us and our clients on the present and the future. But at times you will need to use your already competent skills as a practitioner to look back with the client at unhelpful solutions they have used in the past that keep coming up and blindsiding them.

So what are you waiting for? Let's get building those solutions!

What the dickens is Solution Focused Therapy?

Where do I begin? Let's hear from others first:

Definitions of SFT from literature

'Solution focused brief therapy (SFBT) is a future focused, goal directed approach to brief therapy developed initially by Insoo Kim Berg, Steve De Shazer, and their colleagues and clients at the Milwaukee Brief Family Therapy Centre in the early 1980's.'

De Shazer and Dolan (2007, p1)

'Solution-focused brief therapy is an approach to psychotherapy based on solution-building rather than problem-solving. It explores current resources and future hopes rather than present problems and past causes and typically involves only three to five sessions. It has great value as a preliminary and often sufficient intervention and can be used safely as an adjunct to other treatments.'

Iveson (2002, p149)

'The brief solution focused approach is largely grounded in behavioural, cognitive and cognitive behavioural treatment methods. This approach assumes the goals of counselling are to address and solve current problems in clients' thoughts, behaviour, mood, and physiology. Clinicians using this approach assist clients to expect and pursue positive change. Treatment is semi-structured, focuses on presenting concerns, and combines an eclectic mix of techniques aimed at producing change as efficiently as possible.'

Neukrug and Schwitzer (2006, p208)

'Solution-Focused Brief Therapy is different in many ways from traditional approaches to treatment. It is a competency-based model, which minimizes emphasis on past failings and problems, and instead focuses on clients' strengths and previous successes.'

Trepper *et al* (2010, p1)

'Solution focused brief therapy differs from traditional therapies by eschewing the past in favour of both the present and the future. It is so focused on what is possible that it has little or no interest in gaining an understanding of the problem.'

Corey (2005, p388)

'As the name suggests, it is about being brief and focusing on solutions, rather than on problems.'

Berg (2009)

Overview of Solution Focused Therapy

Solutions not problems

The majority of therapies spend their time focusing on the problem – the nature of the problem, how long it has been present, what are the causes of the problem, has the problem occurred in the past, does this problem cause any other problems, and so forth. I could go on but I think you get the message.

Solution Focused Therapy (SFT) simply shifts the focus from talking about the problem to talking about solutions. Individuals focus on recovering and creating solutions rather than talking about their problems. SFT has little or no interest in gaining an understanding of the problem. The majority of clients know a considerable amount about their problem – they have already been mulling over ways around the problem long before contemplating coming for therapy. SFT believes further examination of the problem to be fruitless.

SFT also believes that there is no need to fully understand the problem in order to find a solution. Take, for example, the internet – something we all tend to take for granted. But how many of us know exactly how it works? When I first started to help my dad use the internet he struggled as he wanted to know exactly what the computer was doing to generate the results it does. Dad was always getting bogged down in trying to understand how it works, which prevented him from using it. But for me it was not about how the solution was being generated, just that it was.

Present and future not the past

Solution Focused Therapy focuses on the present and future rather than the past. Clients are fully aware they are unable to go back and change the past. Some want a better understanding of their past in the belief (hope?) that they can function better in the future. And although I can't deny that this is effective for some people, for others a greater clarity about their past just increases their confusion of how to live now.

The solution may not be related to the problem

This is the part of SFT that many struggle with – both clients and practitioners new to SFT find this part of Solution Focused Therapy the hardest to grasp. I often hear something like, 'Well surely if I have a problem the solution must be to take that problem away and therefore stop it being a problem. How can the solution not be related to the problem?'

Take stress at work as an example. The causes could be numerous – unrealistic demands, unsupportive boss, lack of skills to do the job ... a whole array of factors could contribute to the problem of stress. One way of trying to relieve the stress could be to identify all the contributing factors and then try to do something about them – that is, try to fix each individual stressor and hope that the overall stress reduces. A very sequential, step-by-step, problem-solving approach.

SFT takes a different approach. By eliciting from the client what would be different when the problem was solved, in this case stress, the practitioner works backwards to achieve this goal.

Continuing the above example, suppose the individual states they would spend more time with their family once the problem of stress at work was 'fixed'. SFT works with the individual to see what they could do differently to enable them to spend more time with their family. In this case, the solution is not related to the problem, but helps the individual manage the stress at work more effectively.

And how did it all begin ...

Steve De Shazer and Insoo Kim Berg are credited with developing Solution Focused Brief Therapy (SFBT) together with their colleagues at the Brief Family Therapy Centre in Milwaukee, Wisconsin, USA in the 1980s. Developed inductively rather than deductively, De Shazer and colleagues spent many hours observing a variety of therapy sessions to see what therapist activities were most useful to clients. As a result, SFT is not theory based but developed pragmatically.

De Jong and Berg (2002) note when De Shazer first realised that there was no necessary connection between the problem and the solution. By the end of one session with a particular family, De Shazer and colleagues had listed 27 different problems that had brought the family to therapy. Unable to design an intervention to help, De Shazer asked the family members to focus on something other than the problems, asking them to pay careful attention to 'what is happening in your lives that you want to continue to have happen'. When the family returned two weeks later they said that things were going better and they felt their problems were solved.

Macdonald (2007) reviews how various schools of therapy have influenced SFT. Psychodynamic behaviour therapies and systems therapies all include elements of SFT. Psychodynamic psychotherapy has an emphasis on the client's words, respect for the client's views and no pressure to change. Person Centred Therapy shows confidence in the client's own abilities. Goals and baseline measurements are linked with behaviour therapy. Cognitive therapy highlights client's thoughts and perceptions. Systemic elements include acting 'as if' change has happened. Strategic therapy identified key elements of brief therapy.

As mentioned above, De Shazer and colleagues observed session after session of therapy to see what parts of therapist activity worked for clients. It seems they kept the parts that worked, eliminating the rest. The result is what we know as Solution Focused Therapy.

Key elements of Solution Focused Therapy

Regardless of whether we are incorporating SFT into our work or practising in a strict solution focused way, SFT incorporates the following key elements:

A non-expert, not knowing stance

In SFT the client is seen as the expert and the practitioner takes a stance of not knowing. Lines of enquiry reflect this, with the client leading the conversation and the discussion.

This allows for solutions to develop that are individual to the client. The client is seen as the expert on themselves, with the therapist as expert on facilitating change. Therapists are encouraged to leave their assumptions at the door and listen to how the client sees their lives. Formal theories of thinking, feeling, being, and so forth are discarded, with the emphasis on using the client's language. For example, a Cognitive Behavioural Therapy therapist may identify a thought pattern as 'jumping to conclusions'. In Solution Focused Therapy, the therapist would gently enquire as to what this way of thinking means to the client.

The emphasis on the client's language

As mentioned above, an integral part of Solution Focused Therapy is seeing the client as the expert. As a result of this, the practitioner is encouraged to use the language of the client. Expert 'jargon' is replaced with how the client sees their life.

The requirement that the number of sessions is kept to the minimum necessary

Solution Focused Therapy is a brief therapy, and as such the emphasis is on making the required changes with the client in the least amount of sessions. SFT does not devote time to discovering a reason for the problem(s) or difficulties, but instead focuses on what the client can do in the present to move towards their preferred future. By not focusing on the problem, there is no need for a lengthy assessment, allowing treatment to begin at once.

The value of making changes slowly

Initially this may seem to contradict the above, but SFT values the benefit of the client making any changes slowly. Practitioners are not looking for a monumental change. If change happens quickly then it may be unlikely that the client has developed any solution building skills and will need further support when a similar problem occurs.

Recognition that the problem and the solution are not connected

As mentioned earlier, this always causes difficulties for people new to SFT. But by moving away from problem solving to finding solutions, clients are able to recognise generic solutions that could be used in a variety of problem situations.

Faith in people's abilities, resources and motivation

SFT has a positive belief in people – a belief that they are motivated to change, have the ability to be able to change, and possess the resources necessary to make those changes. When individuals focus solely on their problems, they become de-motivated, lose sight of their great resources, and believe that they lack the ability to do anything about their situation. A practitioner working in a solution orientated way sees the client as containing solutions and not deficits.

No formal theory of change

Unlike other counselling modalities, SFT does not have an elaborative theory behind it. It was simply developed over time by seeing what worked and what did not work for clients in therapy. This can be seen as a help and a hindrance to SFT. A lack of formal theory allows its concepts to be easily learned and practised. But no formal theory makes it harder to test in terms of its effectiveness.

Focus is on the client, not on the expert knowledge of the therapist

The most important person in SFT is the client. SFT is not about the qualifications and experience of the therapist, but how the client sees themselves. The direction of therapy is set by the client. Even if the therapist, in their expert opinion, does not feel that the goals are the correct ones for the client, the simple fact that the goals came from the client means that they are the correct goals.

Box 1.1 Key elements of Solution Focused Therapy

A non-expert, not knowing stance.	The emphasis is on the client's language.
The requirement that the number of sessions be kept to a minimum.	The value of making changes slowly.
Recognition that the problem and the solution are not connected.	Faith in people's abilities, resources and motivation.
No formal theory of change.	Focus is on the client and not on the expert knowledge of the therapist.

Although Solution Focused Therapy has no formal theory behind it, practitioners benefit from adherence to **basic assumptions** and a **central philosophy**.

Basic assumptions

Change is constant and inevitable

No matter what we do or don't do, change will happen. We live in an ever-changing world. SFT recognises this and helps the client to notice what is changing and whether it is cohesive to where they want to be.

Small change leads to bigger change

SFT looks for the smallest of changes. If this change is in the right direction for the client, SFT looks at whether the client can do more of this change. Most clients fail to see the small positive changes that are already occurring. Instead they are expecting a monumental change that will eradicate their problem.

The past cannot be changed

Although a pretty basic assumption, acknowledging that the past cannot be changed is fundamental in SFT. Constantly searching for a resolution to past difficulties distracts from the present and the future that can be influenced.

People have the resources necessary; they are experts on themselves

Once we believe that our clients are the experts on themselves and want what is best for them, we can allow them to navigate as we help them find solutions. Problem focused thinking makes the most resourceful individual impotent as all energies go into examining the problem from different perspectives. SFT has an innate belief that the solutions and resources are in there somewhere. We as practitioners just need to uncover them.

Every human being, relationship and situation is unique

Solution Focused Therapy is unique to each individual. Rarely do we find that a solution that works for one person works for another in exactly the same way. By embracing the uniqueness of each individual, of each relationship and of each situation, we find these unique solutions. It is not a 'one-size-fits-all' therapy, but rather the therapist works with the client to find the precise fit for them.

Every problem has at least one exception

Solution Focused Therapy assumes that no matter how fixed the problem may seem to a client, there is always a time when the problem is not as prominent as it is the rest of the time. I've yet to find someone who reports the same intensity of depression 24 hours a day, 7 days a week. At some time, if only for a fleeting moment, the individual will feel differently. As solution focused practitioners we search for these fleeting moments and notice what's different about them.

Changes come from many directions

As solution focused practitioners we're not fussy as to where the change comes from, as long as it comes. Once we recognise that the solution may not be related to the problem, we can start broadening our horizons to look for anything that could provide us with an exception, a solution, a change. Nothing is filtered out, nothing deemed irrelevant or unimportant.

Box 1.2 Basic assumptions of Solution Focused Therapy	
Change is constant and inevitable.	Small change leads to bigger change.
The past cannot be changed.	People have the resources necessary; they are experts in themselves.
Every human being, relationship and situation is unique.	Every problem has at least one exception.
Changes come from many directions.	

Central philosophy

Simple but pivotal to the workings of Solution Focused Therapy is the central philosophy:

If it ain't broke don't fix it

Solution Focused Therapy's philosophy is to not go looking for problems. If the client has not brought an issue to therapy, it goes against the ethos of SFT to suggest to a client that they should be working on it. By following the key elements and basic assumptions, SFT sees the client as the expert. They are the ones that know what is broken and needs fixing, not the therapist. Only when the client realises that there is a problem does it become a problem. And with that we work with the client to identify exceptions, a preferred future and solutions.

'1 If it ain't broke, DON'T FIX IT!
2 Once you know what works, DO MORE OF IT!
3 If it doesn't work, then don't do it again, DO SOMETHING DIFFERENT!'
(taken from Berg and Miller, 1992)

Once you know what works do more of it

It may seem like simple common sense but, similar to the above, once the client has identified what does work, what solutions do make the problem seem easier, SFT encourages the client to do more of it. The practitioner works with the client to identify their role in making something work. We help the client see what part of the solution they are responsible for; what part they are in control of. But also, and more importantly, how they can make that solution, or part of it, happen again.

'All that is necessary is that the person involved in a troublesome situation does something different'
Steve De Shazer (1985, p7)

If it doesn't work, then don't do it again, do something different

The final part of the philosophy suffers from a case of 'easier said than done'. To start with we don't usually realise that our strategies of old for solving problems aren't working. At one stage they did work, and giving up on that involves the risks associated with doing something different. Not only does the thought of abandoning old coping strategies cause stress, but in the majority of times we don't know what the 'something different' would consist of.

Take, for example, an individual that has always had a couple of drinks to cope with stress. Initially this may have been highly effective – the alcohol would relax the individual and the stress would subside. Over time, as the individual drinks more and more, the original solution becomes part of the problem, but the individual still clings to the hope that their strategy for drinking will work again and relieve stress. As they are so invested in the 'solution', there is a natural reluctance to stop using it.

As SFT practitioners, your job is to help clients realise that their tried and tested methods of solving problems may no longer be working. Once this has been accepted, you move on to the harder task of searching for something different that may work. Although there is no guarantee that the 'something different' will be effective, what we do know is that what the client is currently doing is not working. Helping clients to realise that they will be no worse off by doing something different can help an individual to experiment with alternative ways of solving their problems.

Therapist: Tell me what you've been able to do so far to help with the stress you're experiencing at work?

Client: Well, not much really. When this all started I found relaxing with a few drinks with friends after work really helped. It seems a couple of glasses of wine really helped to take the edge off. Even if there was no one to go out with, I'd buy a bottle on the way home.

Therapist: OK. So wine seemed to really help you relax. And now? Do you find the wine to still be helpful?

Client: Not really. In fact I'm starting to get concerned with how much I've been drinking in the last couple of months. As the stress at work increases I just seem to drink more. And that's now causing me problems – sometimes I struggle to get up in the mornings and a couple of times I've been late for work.

Therapist: So it seems that initially having a couple of drinks really seemed to help you relax – as you said, to take the edge off things. But now the wine seems to be causing you additional problems. I was wondering if you've tried anything else to help with the stress?

Client: Not really. I guess I'm still hoping the wine will help like it used to.

Therapist: What would it be like to maybe stop using the wine as a way to cope with stress and do something else? I'm not sure yet what this 'something else' might look like, but I think if we work together we can come up with something more effective than what you're currently doing to help with your stress.

Applicable to clients and practitioners alike

The central philosophy applies to both clients and therapists when engaging in SFT. As a therapist you need to take note that if what you are doing ain't broke, then don't try to fix it. Similarly, if you know what is working with a client, do more of it. But most importantly, if what you are doing isn't working with a particular client, stop doing it and do something different. If a client isn't doing a particular homework assignment, don't keep asking them to do it, ask them to do something different.

Does it work: how effective is Solution Focused Therapy?

2

The quick and easy answer to this is YES!

If only it was that simple to convince people that it works. Today the emphasis is all on evidence-based practice. The rise of Cognitive Behaviour Therapy (CBT) has been empowered from a strong evidence base that it is effective for a variety of presenting problems.

This section gives a brief outline of the plethora of evidence relating to the effectiveness of Solution Focused Therapy (SFT). A comprehensive description of the evidence can be found in Alasdair Macdonald's (2007) book. As the evidence base on SFT is constantly evolving, a more up-to-date list of studies can be found on Macdonald's (2010) website. The information presented in this section of the book is a snapshot of what I feel summarises the evidence and applications of Solution Focused Therapy. I've tried to show the range of applications that SFT can be used in, but it is only the tip of the iceberg and I would urge anyone interested in a particular area to reference Macdonald's work and, in that way, investigate further.

Overview of effectiveness

Discussion of effectiveness of SFT from literature

'Eighty-nine relevant studies: 2 meta-analyses; 13 randomised controlled trials showing benefit from solution-focused brief therapy with 6 showing benefit over existing methods. Of 30 comparison studies, 23 favour SFT. Effectiveness data are available from more than 3000 cases with a success rate exceeding 60%; requiring an average of 3–5 sessions of therapy time.'

Macdonald (2010)

'There are over 32 published research studies with solution focused brief therapy that show successful outcomes in 65–83% of cases in an average of 4–5 sessions. The highest satisfaction ratings come from the clients themselves. Some of the research studies relate to very serious mental health problems, drug and alcohol use, criminal behaviour and domestic violence.'

Breswick (2009)

'Five studies were well-controlled and all showed positive outcomes – four found SFBT to be better than no treatment or standard institutional services, and one found SFBT to be comparable to a known intervention: Interpersonal Psychotherapy for Depression (IPT).'

Gingerich and Eisengart (2000, p477)

On further examination of the above we see that there is overwhelming evidence outlining that SFT is effective. It is clear that SFT is better than no treatment at all and for some presenting problems it can be better than existing treatments. Not surprisingly, SFT receives high satisfaction ratings from clients – a treatment that looks at clients' strengths and resources and which offers compliments all add to client satisfaction. This higher satisfaction level will keep the client engaged in therapy and help to facilitate change.

Just how brief is brief?

Discussion of brevity of SFT from literature

'Those persons presenting with affective disorders attended an average of 4.14 sessions, with 60.9% partially or mostly resolving their presenting problem. Those who presented with non-affective/relationship problems attended an average of 2.34 sessions, with 76% partially or mostly resolving their presenting problem.'

Reimer and Chatwin (2006, p53)

'The Lambert et al (1998) study, which is the most similar to the current study, reported a mean of 3.1 sessions per client with a mode of 2 sessions. Forty-six percent of the sample were considered recovered after treatment with another 14% considered to be improved, for a total of 60% of the clients considered improved or recovered upon completion of their therapeutic intervention.'

Reimer and Chatwin (2006, p53)

'Stams, Dekovic, Buist, and de Vries (2006) conducted a meta-analysis of 21 international studies including 1421 clients to achieve quantitative evidence for the efficacy of SFBT. They found that although SFBT does not have a larger effect than problem-focused therapy, it does have a positive effect in less time and satisfies the client's need for autonomy more than do traditional forms of psychotherapy.'

Bannink (2007, p90)

The overall consensus from the research indicates that Solution Focused Therapy is brief. Session count is kept to a minimum with problem resolution occurring after the second session for some people.

I can certainly bear witness to this. The first quote above is taken from research where SFT is used in private practice. Those people with whom I take a truly solution focused approach, I have been able to help in a handful of sessions, after which they have turned a corner and have started to do things differently. However, from a business point of view, SFT and '4.14' sessions makes really bad economic sense in private practice!

Solution Focused Therapy and inpatient care

Discussion of SFT and inpatient care from literature

'In the USA, Webster et al. (1994) found evidence that, by using SFT techniques, mental health nurses were able to rethink their philosophy of care and became more focused on helping patients to find solutions to their problems.'

Hosany *et al* (2007, p690)

'The results indicate that both nurses and clients found SFT a helpful approach. Clients reported sessions more focused on their problems. They felt listened to and understood. Following a SFT session, clients talked of feeling uplifted in their mood and there was a sense that clients were more able to look forwards in their lives.'

Stevenson *et al* (2003, p692)

Inpatient care is a constant area of concern for many practitioners, from those that work directly on the wards to practitioners whose clients become inpatients. Some see it simply as 'warehousing', only to be used as a last resort, with little in the way of 'therapy' actually occurring.

SFT seems to be reversing this trend. Nurses who have received only a short, two-day training in SFT techniques show significant increases in the use of these techniques in their patient interactions. Findings from the USA have shown how using a SFT approach has been beneficial for both health care professionals and patients.

Solution Focused Therapy and training and supervision

Discussion of SFT and training and supervision from literature

'A further advantage is that the key principles and therapeutic approaches underpinning SBFT can be integrated into a wide range of psychological models (Trepper et al. 2006). This means that workers do not have to undergo very lengthy and costly training programmes to be able to employ SFBT tools and principles in their clinical practice (Hosany et al. 2007).'

Ferraz and Wellman (2009, p327)

'This paper presents a model of supervision that focuses on supervisee strengths and solutions rather than on problems and mistakes. It discusses how problem-focused supervision can maintain supervisee confusion and shows how the recognition of solutions within one's clinical work can lead to the development of therapeutic competency and clinical self-esteem.'

Wetchler (1990, p129)

Training

The very essence of this book was developed from training that I started to provide to community mental health teams in how to incorporate Solution Focused Therapy into their everyday work. Having worked with Ferraz and Wellman on their initial research on delivering training in SFT to the voluntary sector mental health charity I was working in, I saw first hand how effective SFT techniques can be. Non-therapeutically trained staff could easily incorporate part of SFT into their interactions with clients with very positive effects, not only for clients but also for staff.

Supervision

A substantial part of my clinical supervision involves my supervisor simply telling me to do more of the same. After presenting a particular case, and discussing why I am proceeding the way I am, I am told to continue doing what I am doing. This mirrors part of the central philosophy of SFT – 'if it ain't broke, don't try to fix it'. More importantly, it allows me to build up a conceptual picture of what works in therapy – of what I am doing right.

Using a solution focused stance in supervision can be integral in building up a therapist's sense of what they are doing right in therapy. Focusing on mistakes in supervision increases feelings of inadequacy and confusion. But as Wetchler (1990, p131) states, 'By recognizing successful interchanges with clients, no matter how short lived or seemingly insignificant, the supervisee begins to develop a clinical schema based on success and competency.'

Solution Focused Therapy and specialist applications

Discussion of SFT and inpatient care from literature

*'According to the results of this study, **solution-focused counselling** groups seem to provide a context for student goal achievement, because at least 91% had demonstrated progress toward their goal and 81% of the students achieved their goals at a moderate to very high level.'*

LaFountain and Garner (1996, p136)

*'This study went on to demonstrate what has not been well documented in the literature, namely SFT's effectiveness with **elderly outpatients**. In conclusion, preliminary implications for clinicians indicate that SFT can produce significant clinical outcomes with senior outpatient populations.'*

Dahl *et al* (2000, p45)

*'The experimental group members, on the other hand, were extolled to believe in their own ability to handle the problems associated with **schizophrenia**.'*

Eakes *et al* (1997, p153)

*'This study evaluated the effectiveness of solution-focused brief therapy with **children who have classroom-related behavior problems** within a school setting ... Findings provide support that solution-focused brief therapy was effective in improving internalizing and externalizing behavior problems.'*

Franklin *et al* (2008, p15)

*'Single-session SFBT is a feasible and acceptable intervention for **patients presenting with self-harm** for the first time which can be incorporated into existing psychosocial assessment. The results of this pilot study do not allow us to make a conclusion about its effectiveness, but it does not appear to worsen the outcome.'*

Lamprechet *et al* (2007, p602)

*'In contrast to prevailing treatment approaches that tend to adopt an educative approach, solution-focused therapy's strength-based, minimalist, and client-directed orientation provides an effective alternative for **families coping with suicide** that speaks to the resiliency of families.'*

de Castro and Guterman (2008, p95)

*'Of these, 84% were judged to be improved – 50% reporting abstinence and 34% reporting **controlled drinking** (3 or fewer drinks a day with 2 or more abstinent days per week). Contacts with family members, where available, were used to verify the patient's own reports. De Shazer and Isebaert contrast these findings to those of Polich, Armor, and Braiker (1980) who report a 7% abstinence rate at 4 years for traditional, abstinence-only programs.'*

Trepper *et al* (2006, p135)

The seven quotes above give a taste for how SFT can be effective across a number of areas: in group work; with an elderly population; with individuals diagnosed with schizophrenia; with school children; with individuals who self-harm; in supporting families coping with suicide; and with individuals with an alcohol dependency problem.

Using SFT in groups

SFT is being used more and more in group work. Sharry's (2007) excellent book is an essential addition to any practitioner's tool kit. Elements of SFT are easily incorporated into the majority of groups, something I have been doing for some time in the engagement group I run for individuals with a personality disorder.

More recently, the preliminary results from two pilot groups we have run within Berkshire NHS Foundation Trust have proved very successful in increasing client functioning. These six-week groups used a wholly solution focused approach and took clients being supported by the Alternatives to Admission team who had a variety of problems. As I write, these groups are in the process of being utilised across more localities.

SFT and school children

SFT is increasingly being used with young people, both in and out of a school setting. It seems the key elements, central philosophy and basic assumptions of SFT all gel well with adolescents and children. Treating the young person as the expert instead of telling them what to do, coupled with focusing on the young person's strengths and positive exceptions, aid in creating a strong therapeutic alliance and hence facilitate positive change.

SFT and an elderly population

SFT maintains its effectiveness with an elderly population. Dahl *et al's* (2000) study looked at goal attainment, general patient functioning, motivation and patient satisfaction. The results were consistent with other studies – a significant increase in goal attainment, an average increase of 14 per cent in general level of functioning and high patient satisfaction scores. Notably, in this study, these clinical improvements had been achieved with an average number of sessions as low as 2.3.

SFT and individuals diagnosed with schizophrenia

Eakes *et al* (1997) looked at how family centred SFT can be used to help individuals diagnosed with schizophrenia. Using a systemic approach, the study used the basic assumptions of SFT and assumed family competency, focused on a future when the family will be managing the illness, and built on family strengths by highlighting previous exceptions in coping with and managing difficulties. Results were very encouraging, showing significant differences between the experimental and control groups on expressiveness, active-recreational orientation, moral-religious emphasis and family incongruence.

SFT and individuals who self-harm

Lamprecht *et al* (2007) looked at whether incorporating basic elements of SFT such as the Miracle Question (see section in Chapter 6) and scaling into a full psychosocial assessment could reduce the repeat attendance to a hospital for individuals who self-harm. Results of the pilot study were promising, showing how SFT can be easily incorporated into normal working practices with positive outcomes. From my own experience of working with individuals who self-harm, I have found that searching for exceptions – times when the individual was distressed but did not self-harm – to be very beneficial in reducing incidents of self-harm.

SFT and families coping with suicide

De Castro and Guterman (2008) examined how SFT can be effective with families coping with suicide. By amplifying exceptions of coping, family members can support each other in finding what works in coping with their grief. SFT emphasises the resources and resiliencey families have when faced with such a devastating event. Piercy *et al* (2000) encourage therapists to reframe emotions as strengths, which in turn could be used to develop solutions. This research also highlighted how SFT can be culturally sensitive, echoing one of the key elements of SFT whereby the client is the expert.

Alcohol dependency and SFT

A popular application of SFT has been in the treatment of alcohol and drug dependency. Berg and Miller (1992) and Berg and Reuss (1998) elegantly explain how SFT can be used with this very challenging client group. And the research backs them up – SFT significantly helps individuals reduce their dependency on alcohol or substances.

Behind the research ... what's going on in practice?

Evidence-based treatment refers to therapeutic interventions that have a strong empirical research base to prove that they are an effective treatment for a specific problem. Over the past few years, the prevalence of evidence-based interventions has grown, changing the way that psychological therapy is delivered, which in turn has a knock-on effect on the provision of education and training.

Miller and Duncan start to question our reliance on evidence-based practice:

> *Of late the call has been for the ultimate, all-powerful silver bullet:* the evidence based treatment. *This is the empirically bankrupt notion that for a particular problem, there is a specific treatment that is best. In actuality, to be designated 'evidence based', the developer of a given approach need only prove its superiority to placebo in two studies. Superiority over placebo, however, is not really saying that much; psychotherapy has demonstrated its superiority over placebo for nearly 50 years! Therapy is about twice as efficacious as placebo, and about four times better than no treatment at all. This research, for all its pomp and circumstance, tells us nothing that we already do not know: Therapy works!*
>
> Miller and Duncan (2009; emphasis in original)

In the UK, Cognitive Behaviour Therapy (CBT) is currently seen as the 'silver bullet' of therapy – you would have to be hard pressed to not have noticed the onslaught of CBT books and training courses on offer. CBT is in favour as it has a strong evidence base showing that it can be effective for a range of problems compared to no treatment at all. However, it is crucial to remember that the research does not show CBT to be better than other psychological treatments; simply that it is better than placebo.

Solutions from the USA

SFT was born and bred in the USA. It was welcomed by health insurance companies as it provided significant positive outcomes in a limited number of sessions. As Aronson put it:

> *HMOs [Health Maintenance Organisations] here love solution focused therapy as it tends to be short term and therefore cheaper for them ... when I was applying for credentialing with various HMO's most of them want to know if you're trained in SFBT. Clearly it's a priority for them.*
>
> (Aronson, 2009)

My experience of being insured by an HMO when living in the USA really brings this home. Most plans I looked at will provide cover for six sessions of psychological therapy, after which time the practitioner needs to justify the need for further sessions. My training in the USA responded to this demand – brief therapy is taught as a way to keep session count to a minimum to ensure reimbursement. With the public purse being stretched to its limit, maybe the UK government needs to take a fresh look at why SFT is so popular with HMOs in the USA.

Summary and the future of Solution Focused Therapy

Trepper *et al* give us the best summary of the research:

> *Although there has not been a plethora of well-controlled, clinical trial studies of the effectiveness of SFBT, those that have been done, along with the smaller, clinically-based and quasi-experimental studies, suggest that SFBT: (a) is more effective than no treatment (Lindforss & Magnusson, 1997; Newsome, 2004; Zimmerman et al., 1996); (b) is at least as effective as current psycho-social treatments (Gingerich & Eisengart, 2000); (c) in some cases and/or for some problems may be more effective than problem-focused treatments (Cockburn, Thomas, & Cockburn, 1997; La Fountain & Garner, 1996; Lambert et al, 1998; Springer, Lynch & Rubin, 2000); and (d) in most cases, shows significantly fewer sessions to achieve similar outcomes (Littrell, Malia & Vanderwood, 1995).*
>
> (Trepper *et al*, 2006, p136)

Practitioners can be confident that not only is SFT effective, but it can be so in less time than more traditional ways of working. Other evidence shows how staff seem able to make good utilisation of the key elements of SFT after only a relatively short training.

Its effectiveness on clients seems unquestionable. But its effects on staff also needs further research – my initial impression, and one borne out in the research by La Fountain and Garner (1996), is that SFT lends itself to lower staff burnout rates compared with staff who always focus on problems.

Another overwhelming conclusion from nearly all of the studies was a call for further research. As Professor Wellman elegantly mentions in the Foreword of this book, Solution Focused Therapy is always the bridesmaid but never the bride. Professionals from a plethora of different specialisms rave about how effective SFT can be in working with a wide variety of populations, but rarely is it given top billing over other therapies. SFT is yet to make the headlines.

However, things seem to be changing in the USA. The Solution Focused Brief Therapy Association's website states that SFT is being listed with other evidence-based programmes:

> *Solution Focused Brief Therapy has been officially listed in the Office of Juvenile Justice's Model Programs Guide, with other evidence-based programs. SFBT has been rated 'Promising', which is the first of three possible ratings, based on the number and strength of the empirical research supporting it. This is an important step in SFBT's acceptance as an evidenced-based approach. As you may know, some agencies are beginning to review treatment models and programs and decide whether they meet their criteria for being 'evidence-based'.*
>
> (Solution Focused Brief Therapy Association website, 2009)

I feel the best of Solution Focused Therapy is yet to come.

The power of the therapeutic relationship

Regardless of the type of therapy being used, if as practitioners we cannot form a therapeutic relationship with the client the best interventions will struggle to have any significant impact. Corey (2005) sees counselling as a personal matter that involves a personal relationship, stating that evidence indicates that honesty, sincerity, acceptance, understanding and spontaneity are basic ingredients for successful outcomes.

'Determine that the thing shall be done, and then we shall find the way.'
Abraham Lincoln

According to Haugh and Paul (2008), the centrality and importance of the therapeutic relationship has been replicated in more than 1,000 studies. They cite Wampold (2001), who examined what works in therapy, identifying that general effects (common factors that underlie all psychotherapies) account for 70 per cent of the outcomes of therapy, specific effects (particular aspects linked to a specific model) account for 8 per cent, and unexplained variability account for 22 per cent.

Lambert (1992) reviewed many studies that try to identify some of the common factors that work in therapy. The four most common factors identified are extratherapeutic change, hope and expectancy, model or technique used, and therapeutic relationship. Further developments of this research cite the therapeutic relationship as being responsible for up to 30 per cent of positive outcomes in therapy (Assay and Lambert, 1999).

These findings are discussed in McKergow and Korman (2009). Rather than downplaying the importance of the therapeutic model, the authors state that: 'We propose that models featuring complicated and explanatory mechanisms and psychological explanations may require excessive efforts in terms of both therapist training and practice. However, the extent to which the SFBT approach leaves aside many psychological explanations and assumptions is remarkable.' The therapeutic relationship is thus strengthened by the ease of understanding the client has of the model as they realise that there is nothing hidden or secretive to the process of change.

What is the therapeutic relationship?

One definition of the therapeutic relationship is that it includes all the variables that are found in therapy regardless of the therapist's theoretical orientation, such as empathy, warmth and acceptance (Haugh and Paul, 2008). More simply, however, I see it as how we as practitioners relate to our clients; it is the working alliance we create with them, the rapport we have with them, the understanding that we elicit from them about how they see their world, and how we collaborate with them to find solutions.

My initial introduction to the world of counselling and therapy was heavily influenced by the works of Carl Rogers (1951) and person-centred counselling. Rogers' core conditions of unconditional positive regard, congruence and empathy accompany me in every interaction with clients. These core conditions seem to be universal in every model or technique cited in the literature. All that seems to vary is how different approaches use the therapeutic relationship to help the client change (see Corey, 2005, pp478–9)

Hall and Marzillier (2009, p407) note that 'a strong working alliance is necessary whatever techniques are used'. With SFT being seen as a brief intervention, there is increasing pressure to develop a strong working alliance and therapeutic relationship as soon as possible.

How Solution Focused Therapy influences the therapeutic relationship

Solution Focused Therapy enhances the therapeutic relationship in many subtle ways. Every aspect of the philosophy, principles and techniques are designed to strengthen the working alliance between the client and the therapist, as detailed below:

Solution Focused Therapy and the therapeutic relationship

Non-problem talk

As discussed elsewhere in this book, Solution Focused Therapy involves something called non-problem talk. This involves getting the client outside of the problem. Clients have a tendency to only want to talk about the problem. By making a concerted effort to get to know the person behind the problem, the client feels listened to, resulting in a stronger therapeutic relationship. Non-problem talk also allows for limited self-disclosure by the practitioner, something that can be instrumental in developing the therapeutic relationship.

Use of compliments

A large part of SFT involves the use of compliments, as we shall see in Chapter 6 (Building solutions). Genuine compliments help the client to see that the practitioner is on their side and can make the client feel accepted. And let's face it – someone telling you how good you are, how well you are coping, and who can see in you the strengths and resources that you thought had disappeared, is bound to do wonders for the therapeutic relationship.

Client as the expert

As we saw earlier in the book, SFT sees the client as the expert on themselves, not the therapist. With the balance of power leaning more towards the client, the relationship is seen as a more equal one, allowing the client and practitioner to work together to find the solutions that are best for the client.

Use of the client's words

SFT emphasises the importance of using the client's words. In using the terminology and language generated by the client, not only does the client feel listened to, but it also shows great respect for what the client is saying.

Importance of the client's goals and preferred future

In all that it does, SFT relies on the client to generate how they see their future and what it is they want to work on. This in itself strengthens the relationship as it emphasises that it is the client's unique agenda that is important and that the practitioner is not using a 'one-size-fits-all' therapy.

Provide structuring

SFT relies heavily on a series of questions, providing the client with structure. These questions take away the initial need for the client to simply 'talk'. There is no pressure to constantly put difficult feelings and emotions into words. There are not the heavy silences where the client can feel lost as to what might be going on.

Respectful to the client

Many therapies utilise a concept of 'resistance', which assumes that if the client is not making progress then they are failing to cooperate for conscious or unconscious reasons. This absolves the responsibility of the therapist and explicitly blames the client. In SFT, there is no such thing as resistance, just the client's unique way of cooperating. SFT sees it as the therapist's role to engage with the client in such a way that will facilitate change. If the client didn't do a task, the fault is with the task and its timing or presentation, not with the client.

I'm very much aware that other therapy modalities could come up with a similar list of how their model enhances the therapeutic relationship. This isn't meant to be a competition. But for me there is something about Solution Focused Therapy that just hits the mark. I feel it's a combination of the open therapeutic style, the way SFT involves working in partnership with clients and the way it enhances clients' strengths and confidence.

Without a doubt, SFT is a positive therapy. But it's more than that. Clients seem to want to come back and engage in therapy – they want to discover more of their strengths and resources; they want to find more solutions. Conversations centred on solutions are always preferable to those focused on problems. And with these solutions there is more of an opportunity to develop a sense of fun, a sense of humour into the therapy room, integral in relationship development.

Lazarus (1996) views the client–therapist relationship as the soil that enables the therapist's techniques to take root. This is true across all relationships, no matter what type of work you are in. If you cannot develop a relationship with the individual you are working with, your skills and knowledge will fail to have the impact you had hoped for. Embracing the tools, techniques and philosophy of Solution Focused Therapy will enable you to make that relationship a firm foundation on which to facilitate change.

How change happens

There are many modalities of psychological therapy available and just as many different ways of supporting people. The one thing they have in common is that they are trying to facilitate change. But just how does change happen?

> 'One consequence of a changing, polarity-based system is the reality of conflict and struggle. Everything in the Universe grows and changes through a process of struggle and conflict, leading to clarity and understanding, and then back to conflict, struggle and change again. The Elders told us that is a natural part of growth and a natural part of an interconnected system. We usually hate it when the conflict begins. But the teaching says, "When the struggle starts, get happy." It means a change is starting to occur. If there's no struggle, the odds aren't too good that anything of significance is going to occur. They taught us that conflict is a friend, not an enemy. Struggling is part of growing. If we find ourselves out of harmony, we often need to struggle to get back to it. Conflict is a guidance system, it's a friend.'
>
> *Don Coyhis (2000, p91)*

Although Solution Focused Therapy (SFT) doesn't have a formal theory behind how it works, I feel it integral to any book on therapy to look at how change happens. No matter what your role is, if you are reading this book you will no doubt be looking at implementing change either for the individuals you support or for yourself. By simply reading this book a change will start to occur.

Formal theories of change by Prochaska and DiClemente (1982) suggest that different interventions need to be used dependent on which stage of change the client has reached. These stages are seen as pre-contemplation, contemplation, preparation, action, maintenance and termination. Macdonald (2007) recognises preparation, action, maintenance and termination as being particularly useful for SFT, noting that when clients are not ready for change, solution focused therapy can become more solution forced.

Further examination of the stages of change

Preparation

Getting ready to change can be as important as the change itself. Understanding why we are making a change is a key part of working out how change happens. If we are engaged with the change process, if we know why we are making a change, we are more likely to make the change a reality. Clients are more likely to follow through on doing something differently if they come up with the idea themselves. Working on the premise that the client is the expert, they, and they alone, know why they need to make a change.

Envisaging a preferred future is crucial in preparing for any change – seeing how life would be after these changes have been made can be the catalyst for change. With that preferred future must come a belief that the change will make a positive difference.

Motivation and readiness to change are also fundamental in preparing for change. Carey *et al* (2007) learned that when clients reached 'rock bottom' or realised that 'enough was enough', they decided that it was time to make a change. Realising that they are in a place they do not want to be in can be the motivation to change. Clients who present on their own accord to therapy generally have reached that point where they feel something needs to be different – they are ready to start to do something different.

The final part of preparation comes in evaluating the resources needed to make change happen. Do we have the skills, abilities and resources within ourselves or do we need to search for them externally? Does the change to reach our goals involve gaining extra resources?

Action – what changes?

Carey *et al* (2007) identify three main areas of change – actions, feeling and thinking. Changing can involve the start of doing something differently or may involve something we haven't tried before. This can lead to a change in how we perceive ourselves, and a change in how we feel. Simply by changing our behaviour, changes in our thinking and feelings can follow.

Changing how we think can involve changing our attitudes towards ourselves or others, accepting character traits or situations as they are, or reframing a situation and seeing it in a different way. Carey *et al* (2007) found changes in feelings related to changes in emotional states such as depression, self-esteem, guilt, anger and aggressiveness. Changes tended to be in the direction of being more tolerant, relaxed, calm, chilled out and happy.

Changes can come from many directions. We can use our internal resources to do something or to think in a different way. Or the change can be externally influenced – something someone says can help us realise resources and qualities we didn't know we had. A genuine compliment can be internalised leading to a change in how we feel about ourselves or a situation.

Gaining tools and strategies and learning more about themselves were two key factors identified by Carey *et al* (2007) in their research. They found that by using various tools and strategies such as relaxation, activity charts, information and homework set by the therapist, clients felt in greater control of their situation. In SFT, encouraging the client to do something different can also facilitate an increase in their sense of control – clients start to feel more in the driving seat of their lives rather than a passenger to the way they feel and the problems they are experiencing.

Maintenance

Once the change has began, how do we keep it going? What makes us persevere when our initial efforts don't seem to bring us anywhere closer to our goals and that preferred future?

Positive reinforcement plays a significant role in changing. Setting small, achievable goals allows us to experience success, fuelling motivation for us to continue doing something differently. Some changes require perseverance – change happens when we stick with something rather than giving up at the first obstacle. As the quote at the start of this section outlines, if we can change without struggle then the change may not be worth having.

Support from others can be vital in maintaining change. Simple recognition of changes we are making and encouragement can help keep us on track. It's easier to get fit with someone coaching you. It's easier to try new things, experiment a little, with some back up. Personal growth is easier with others involved. Solution Focused Therapy is in itself relational – we encourage our clients to see how a change would look from someone else's viewpoint. Involving others in our change increases the possibility that we will reach our goals.

Termination – when is enough enough?

What tells us when we have changed enough? Is it when we have reached our goals and are experiencing our preferred future, or is it when we no longer have to constantly do something different in order to maintain our current level of functioning?
I could argue that we are an ever-changing species; that change is inevitable no matter what we do. But termination in relation to psychological therapy looks at when the goal that was decided has been reached and has been maintained – the change has become a permanent fixture in an individual's everyday functioning.

All at once or little by little

When change happens, does it happen suddenly or gradually? It seems the jury is split on this.

Theories of change suggest that change is a gradual progress. Prochaska and DiClemente (1982) and Prochaska and Norcross (2001) describe a very definite process of change. In this vein, in her description of the grieving process Kübler-Ross (1969) outlines the transition curve, and how we go through stages of grieving in order to cope with the change brought on by loss.

But people's accounts of how change happens seem to contradict this idea of a step-by-step process. Carey *et al* (2007) asked clients to describe change and in doing so learned that clients seem to experience change both as a gradual process and as something that just happens. As one participant in their study mentioned: 'It was gradual but the realization was sudden.' It seems that although the actual process of change may be gradual, the recognition that a change has happened may be a sudden one.

Sometimes we're too close to a situation to see that things are changing. We expect big, dramatic changes that will alter our lives, but in reality change tends to happen in small doses. Even when the change is sudden, such as a promotion at work, it can take a few months until we start to assimilate that change into how we feel.

Take losing weight for example. The other day I saw an old client who I hadn't seen for about a year. One of the first things she said was, 'Have you lost weight?' (Compliments are always a great start to any therapy session if you ask me!) To be honest, I was unsure how to answer. I supposed that I had lost weight, but to me it had been a very gradual progress of a few pounds over an extended period of time. But to someone who hadn't seen me for a while, I guess the change was more noticeable.

As much as I'd like to keep going on about my weight loss, the point of my little story is that change isn't instantaneous. Like weight loss, we have to work at it in a number of ways. Rarely does it just happen. There may be a defining moment for some of what they feel needs to change, but the process itself is usually slow.

But at the same time, how our individual client perceives change is of utmost importance. If we as practitioners try to inflict our educated theories of change on to an individual who feels that change just happens, we may be fighting a losing battle. Change is different for different people. Your job as practitioners is to find the process of change that meets the client's needs. Work with them to set achievable goals that relate to a preferred future. Help them realise their true resources. And steer them into doing something different.

Solution Focused Therapy and change

Solution Focused Therapy is all about helping our clients realise the changes that they feel are best for them. Part of the key elements of SFT is recognising the value of making changes slowly. SFT does not have a formal theory of change but instead recognises the client as the expert in knowing the type of change and the process of change that is right for them.

'Growth means change, and change involves risk, stepping from the known to the unknown.'
George Shinn (n.d.)

Some of the *basic assumptions* of Solution Focused Therapy relate to change. SFT sees change as inevitable; small changes lead to big change and changes come from many directions. The central philosophy of SFT is if something doesn't work, don't do it and do something different. The something different is the change that the client is looking to make. Box 4.1 summarises how SFT looks at change.

Box 4.1 Solution Focused Therapy and change

Key elements of SFT	Values making change slowly. Client as the expert – clients know what change is best for them.
Basic assumptions of SFT	Change is inevitable. Small changes lead to big changes. Changes come from many directions.
Central philosophy of SFT	If it's not working, stop doing it and do something different.

As SFT practitioners we work with our clients to help them prepare for change – we help them see their resources, both internal and external. Being engrossed in a problem can lead to blinkered thinking – all thoughts and resources are related to trying to solve the problem. Helping our clients see the whole picture of themselves can enable them to be ready to make a change.

SFT works with the client to find that preferred future. As we will see later in this book, the Miracle Question (see Chapter 6) can help the client clarify where they would like to see their lives go. From that we encourage them to start taking the small steps towards that preferred future, helping them set achievable goals and experiment to find out what the 'doing something different' might entail.

As solution focused practitioners we need to work with our clients to identify all possible sources of change and how we can maximise them. We work with our clients to reframe the way they see themselves, generating some of the changes in their thinking and feeling. We work with our clients to see what they can stop doing that isn't working. We work to help them identify the exceptions to when that change might be already happening. We compliment our clients when they have managed to make a change, no matter how small. And we use scaling to help them see whether they have made enough change.

And when we've done all that, we ask, 'What else?' to see where the client wants to go next.

Being more solution focused helps us to really look into how change happened and why. By doing that we can try to come up with an answer to the question, 'How does change happen?' And the majority of the time the answer will be unique – the way I try to make change happen will be different from the next person. Neither of us is wrong. No one is better than the other.

Box 4.2 Summary of tools for change in Solution Focused Therapy

Stage of change	Tools in SFT	Examples of change focused questions
Preparation	Search for client resources. Preferred future – the Miracle Question. Goal setting.	What is it that you could use to help make this change? When this change has been made, what is it that you see as being different in your life?
Action	Behavioural experiments. Exceptions. Reframing.	How do you think things would be different if you tried relaxing every day instead of just once a week? Are there times when you've felt some of these changes have occurred already?
Maintenance	Compliments. Relational questions. Scaling.	How could you maintain this change? Who else has noticed that a change has started to happen? That sounds like a great change – how did you manage to do that? If you are currently at an eight on your scale of where you want to be, what would being a nine look like?

From problems to solutions: changing the focus of the practitioner

The biggest task I face when training other professionals about Solution Focused Therapy (SFT) is in getting them to put their focus on problems to one side. The majority of professionals have been trained to focus on problems and to then work with clients to alleviate those problems. Probably the most dominant model in mental health is the medical model where we move from assessment to diagnosis to treatment. Professionals in this context are seen as the experts – we are the ones who will fix your problem.

'A visitor arrived inquiring about Zen. Master Nan-in (1868–1912) silently poured him a cup of tea and continued pouring until the cup overflowed. "Why do you continue to pour after the cup is full?" asked the visitor. "To show you," replied the Nan-in, "that you are like this cup: so full of your own preconceptions that nothing can go in. I can't tell you about Zen until you have emptied your cup."'

Taken from Winokur (1989, p55)

I was one of those professionals. My initial training in psychology and counselling taught me to focus on the problem, and I too struggled when first presented with SFT. It's not easy to work in a way that goes against years of training and experience. Listening for solutions, exceptions, resources and strengths requires a totally different frame of mind from traditional ways of working. The focus is changed to see strengths rather than deficits.

Practitioners seem to struggle to throw caution to the wind, take that leap of faith, and stop paying so much attention to the problem. I guess it feels wrong not to ask problem-solving questions. It feels a little like we're short-changing our clients. Here they are, coming to us for help with their problems, and all we want to do is talk about solutions. How can this be right?

The protests I hear are numerous. The loudest being, 'What about the risk assessment?' Risk assessments are commonplace in statutory services with what can seem like an ever increasing demand for the management of risk over the therapeutic needs of the client. Seasoned practitioners in SFT such as Berg and De Shazer elegantly determine the level of risk from their therapeutic interview. But the purpose of this book is not to encourage you to discard your good practice for the search for solutions, but rather to embrace its ideas into your practice.

Problem focused versus solution focused

Box 5.1 highlights some of the differences between being solution focused and problem focused. Again this is not meant as a criticism of problem focused ways of working, but simply as a way to bring to your attention how different ways of working may affect the conversations you have with clients.

Box 5.1 Problem focused versus solution focused

Problem focused	Solution focused
Interest in the past.	Interest in the present and future.
Goals of the service.	Client's goals.
Expert is the expert.	Client is the expert.
Deficits.	Resources and strengths.
Disability.	Ability.
Pathology.	Competence.
Resistance.	Cooperation.

Conversations that discuss problems differ considerably from those in which we talk about solutions. Once we start in a problem focused way, it can be difficult to move the conversation to one where we want to talk about strengths, resources and solutions. One of your tasks as practitioners is to steer the language of the conversation to one that facilitates the discussion of solutions. Box 5.2 highlights these differences.

Box 5.2 The language of problems and solutions

Language of problems	Language of solutions
What I *don't* want.	What I *do* want.
When things *go wrong*.	When things *go right*.
Forces *beyond* my control.	Forces *within* my control.
I'm *stuck*.	I am *progressing*.
I expect *more troubles* to come.	I see some positive *possibilities*.

Before you get started searching for solutions with your clients, I encourage you to start using some of the techniques I have mentioned in order to change your focus from problems to solutions. The following exercises should expedite that shift.

Discovering your best self

This exercise is highly versatile for both practitioner training and for use with clients. For practitioners it allows them to think differently about themselves, allowing them to experience what it may be like to be on the receiving end of questions designed to find solutions and strengths. For clients it can be a simple way to get them to think about how they are when they are at their best. From these answers we can see if they can be encouraged to do more of what makes them feel good about themselves.

When using this exercise with clients caution needs to be used if they have had a difficult or abusive childhood. Asking them to recap on their childhood may be counterproductive as the good times may be overshadowed by the struggles they experienced.

Don't be surprised if you or your clients struggle to fill out some of the boxes. Being focused on negatives and problems for so long can make it difficult to see the positives in yourself and your clients. Sometimes doing this exercise with someone who knows you well can help you uncover something about yourself that may have become hidden over the years.

Exercise: discovering your best self

What are your greatest achievements? What would your best friend say they might be?

What skills, talents and abilities shine out in you?

What are you passionate about?

What did you like to do as a child? What are your memories of having fun?

What do you like best about yourself?

What is true of you when you are at your best?

Looking for exceptions in our clients: seeing beyond the problem

When clients present to us engulfed in their problems, we can struggle to see past their problems and notice anything else. To some extent, this is what they want – if all we see is their problem it may increase the chance of us solving it. Even when we've been working with a client for a length of time, we may lose sight that there are many other facets to the person other than their problem. This simple exercise encourages you to see more than just that problem. And in answering these questions you might get an insight into possible solutions within your clients.

Exercise: looking for exeptions in our clients

Think of three things you admire about a client you are working with despite the difficulties of the case.

Think of five non-problem related things about your client.

Think of five positive things you have done to help the client.

The strengths within us

Clients can find it hard to see their strengths and resources. After drowning in their problems for so long, encouraging them to see what's good within them can seem very alien.

This exercise starts to help you look for solutions instead of problems by identifying solutions in your own work. Often we become so bogged down in the pressures of our work we forget to take a step back and see just how good we are. When we start to do a job we're very much aware of the skills needed to complete the task, drawing on our recent training or experience from other areas of our lives. The more we do a job, the less recognition we give ourselves – solving problems becomes automatic.

Opening ourselves up to how our own resources are used to create solutions within our jobs helps us see solutions in the people we work with. It's easy to get stuck with our own problems, but looking at how we find solutions to problems will help us empower others to find solutions for themselves.

This exercise allows you to experience what it is to look at yourself through a positive lens. It encourages you to break down what it is you are good at in your job. Try to answer one of these questions for as many strengths as possible. Hopefully once completed, you will get a better picture of how Solution Focused Therapy can work, and add to your belief in your own job skills.

Exercise: the strengths within us

What is one of your strengths at work?

What is it that you do that makes this a strength?

What is it that you do differently from your colleagues?

What would your clients say you do well?

How would you know if you were doing your job better?

Is there anything other people do that you could incorporate into your work?

What do you feel you need in order to be a little better at your job?

Leaving your assumptions at the door

It can be hard to go into any interaction with a client without having a whole host of preconceived ideas about them and their problems and what brings them to therapy. Be it in the form of an official referral letter or from the initial phone call when arranging an appointment, rarely do we see a client without knowing something about them.

'Until we lose ourselves there is no hope of finding ourselves.'
Henry Miller
Quoted in Winokur (1989, p66)

We can all describe the general characteristics of someone who is depressed, but by doing so we miss the person behind the diagnosis. Instead of listening and observing and finding out about the client in front of us we sometimes use our own perceptions, baggage, experiences and training to cloud what the client may be telling us. As a result, we won't be finding out about *their* solution.

An integral part of SFT is adopting a stance of not knowing. Take the word 'depressed' as an example. As a practitioner you probably have a pretty good working knowledge of what being depressed entails. But what does being depressed mean to the individual in front of you? Neither of you is 'right', but in SFT the client is the expert so we use their words, their meaning of what it is to be depressed.

Once you have a working definition of what being depressed means to the individual in front of you, ask more questions of yourself and your client to expand on their meaning. For example, what would I see you doing when you're this depressed? What would your partner see you doing? What would you be thinking? The dialogue below highlights the two ways of asking about depression – problem focused and solution focused:

Problem focused:

Therapist: Thank you for coming to see me today. What seems to be the problem?

Client: Nothing in my life is going well. I feel so depressed.

Therapist: Could you tell me a little more about your depression. How has your sleep been?

Client: Terrible. I just lie awake desperate to get some sleep.

Therapist: And your appetite?

Client: It's gone. I can't remember the last time I ate a proper meal.

Therapist: OK. And are you managing to do anything during the day at the moment?

Client: No, nothing. I spend most of the day in bed trying to sleep. I haven't even managed to have a shower for the last few days.

In the above example, the therapist is asking questions about the client's depression related to the diagnostic criteria for depression. Using their 'expert' knowledge of depression, the therapist is focusing on the problem to see if the client's understanding of 'depression' matches the symptoms for a diagnosis of depression.

Solution focused:

Therapist: What is it that brings you to see me today?

Client: Nothing in my life is going well. I feel so depressed.

Therapist: That must be really tough. I see lots of people with depression and everyone tells me something different. Would you be able to tell me what being depressed means to you?

Client: I'll try. Well for the last few weeks I've struggled to get out of bed to do anything. I just don't seem to have the energy to do anything any more. Sometimes crying for no reason. I don't know why I stay in bed – I can't seem to sleep. I think I've been losing weight – I'm certainly not eating. And I just seem so sad all the time.

Therapist: OK. Thank you. When you're not in bed, what might I see you doing even though this depression seems to have taken over?

Client: Not much really. Sometimes I manage to have a bath but I used to be able to do that every day. And sometimes I can watch TV with my partner.

Therapist: And your partner. What are they noticing that's different about you since you've been depressed?

Client: He's not seen me smile or laugh for ages. I think that must be the biggest change. He could always make me laugh, even when I've been really upset.

In the solution focused approach, the therapist is able to acquire the same information about appetite, sleep and energy levels, but does it by allowing the client to describe in their own words how they are experiencing their depression. The client also lets slip some exceptions to their depression – times when it might not be as bad. And indirectly we have a goal – for the client to laugh and smile with their partner again.

Exercise: leaving your assumptions at the door

Start exploring how your concepts and definitions of everyday words, tasks and activities may differ from those of the people around you. Simply knowing that others may see things differently from you will enhance your listening skills and help you see the client as the expert. Use friends, family, partners and colleagues to do this task – the broader range of people you use, the more you will learn!

Below is an example, but try to think of as many different concepts as you can.

Word/Concept/Activity: Respect		
My definition	Dictionary/Internet definition	Definition according to three other people
A positive feeling towards another person whereby we value their opinions, values and abilities.	Esteem for or a sense of worth or excellence of a person, a personal quality or ability, or something considered as a manifestation of a personal quality or ability (http://dictionary.reference.com/browse/respect	1. Valuing another persons qualities, opinions, and abilities 2. Looking up to someone 3. Consideration for other people

Word/Concept/Activity:		
My definition	Dictionary/Internet definition	Definition of three other people

Stuck at what else to explore ...? What about being happy, doing the washing up, confidence, having a shower, love.

Once you have successfully mastered the above, you can start looking at examples closer to the client group you support. For example, take a diagnosis and start looking for evidence for and against the assumptions you have about that disorder. With the clients you are currently working with, start searching for exceptions and additions to the diagnostic criteria you've been working from. Start seeing the client behind the label.

The person behind the label	
How I see *depression*	How my client sees *depression*

The person behind the label	
How I see *being bullied*	How my client sees *being bullied*

The person behind the label	
How I see being a *victim of abuse*	How my client sees being a *victim of abuse*

The person behind the label	
How I see	How my client sees

This exercise can work for any particular area where your own assumptions may be preventing you from seeing more than just the client's problem. Your own definition of a particular label will be based on diagnostic standards and your own experience and training. It may be the same as the client's meaning. Only by seeing the client as the expert will you find out.

Solution scavenger hunt

Exercise: solution scavenger hunt

This is a really simple and fun exercise adapted from Fiske and Zalter (2005). It was originally designed for use within training workshops to help trainees to identify and utilise some of the components of SFT. I've used this exercise as a homework assignment for practitioners learning about SFT between training days but also as a homework assignment for clients who are struggling to see solutions.

Start searching for solutions in the world around you. Find a story, picture, performance, piece of documentary evidence, newspaper article, song or TV programme that highlights any of the concepts covered in SFT. Use examples of your current work or your colleague's work. Top marks if you can find evidence of a miracle!

Pay special attention to examples of:

- compliments
- miracles
- how a change has happened or may happen
- a person's unique solution to a problem
- a positive, solution focused song
- what was different when someone (a client, colleague, you, anyone) surprised you by recovering more quickly than expected
- any company or organisation offering 'solutions'
- an exception
- evidence of strengths and resources
- someone meeting their goals or targets.

Keep this scavenger hunt going for as long as you can. Keeping an eye out for solutions in the world around you will help you when searching for specific solutions with your clients.

What do practitioners like about Solution Focused Therapy?

Once practitioners have got over the initial awkwardness of focusing on solutions, the feedback received shows how Solution Focused Therapy appeals to individuals across many disciplines. Strong and Nielsen examined how counsellors felt about using SFT. They found that:

> *In response to being asked about the experience of asking the miracle question, counsellors offered responses that described how asking it helped to explore the 'uniqueness of clients and ideas and circumstances', 'the idiosyncrasies of their needed solutions', and so on.*
>
> (Strong and Nielsen, 2008, p255)

Strong and Nielson (2008) examined all types of counselling interventions, and found that counsellors preferred those interventions prevalent in SFT, such as exploring and adopting the perspectives of clients, identifying alternative perspectives, identifying strengths, possibilities and solutions, and developing a shared understanding.

Hogg and Wheeler (2004) looked at what social workers value about using Solution Focused Therapy within their work. Overall their research pointed to a very positive evaluation of SFT as an adjunct to their practice skills. Box 5.3 highlights what Hogg and Wheeler found to be most useful to social workers when using SFT.

Box 5.3 What social workers find most useful about SFT

Helps practitioner to engage with children/young people and carers under a range of circumstances.
Focusing on what is working automatically points to what is not.
Identifying small steps for change can result in immediate progress and is great for relationship building.
It is an approach that can be easily adapted for frontline service, requiring only a short period of training.
Offers the potential for a common language across professionals (for example, using scaling).
Provides the facilitator with a clearer picture of what is happening in the client's life.
Generates goals for work that are more likely to be owned by clients and sustained over time.

Cont.

Box 5.3 What social workers find most useful about SFT

Brings client's resources to the fore.

Strengthens relationships with family and friends.

Helps clients to manage without professional support.

Helps to organise the work around the uniqueness of clients.

As well as the above, the researchers found that scaling questions allowed social workers to acquire a lot of information very quickly and that social workers saw problem-free talk as being invaluable in their work: 'It can be a relief and liberating'; 'Something different to talk about'; 'You learn a lot more when you aren't asking about problems' (quoted in Strong and Nielson, 2008, p257).

What's best for practitioners?

In a recent email debate on the United Kingdom Association for Solution Focused Practice website, solution focused practitioners were asked to highlight which parts of SFT they value the most. The list included:

- Moving forward is possible.
- If it ain't broke don't try to fix it.
- It's a 'way of thinking'.
- Staying curious.
- Belief that everyone is competent.
- Client as the expert.
- Their best hopes for the session.
- Dealing in solutions increases practitioner resilience.
- Resistance as curiosity.

(personal communication, UK Association for Solution Focused Practise Forum, www.ukasfp.co.uk, 2/2/2009)

Similarities were found in the research by De Shazer and Dolan (2007) on how therapists experience SFT. They found that therapists had a renewed interest in their work and experienced less burnout. Therapists also found that SFT suggests a more equal partnership between client and therapist with the therapist not burdened with the responsibility of change. Attendance by clients increased when focusing on solutions rather than problems, with clients willing to work harder when their areas of strengths were acknowledged.

LaFountain and Garner (1996) researched what difference running groups in a solution focused way made to school counsellors. They found at the one year follow-up of their research that significant differences could be seen in the emotional exhaustion and depersonalisation between those counsellors who had used solution focused methodology and those who had not. One of the conclusions of the study seemed to be that the use of solution focused groups resulted in lower levels of stress and burnout in counsellors.
My own and my colleagues' experience in using SFT reiterates the findings of LaFountain and Garner (1996), both with groups and individuals. Searching for strengths, resources and solutions allows me to manage a large caseload effectively. I believe incorporating SFT into all aspects of my work is fundamental in maintaining my own mental health when working with some of the most damaged and challenging individuals that present for psychological therapy.

Common barriers to use

As much as the ideas presented in this book are well received by professionals, there tends to be some reluctance to actually start to use them. Below are some of the more common reasons I come across that get in the way of incorporating solution focused ideas into everyday work:

Professional culture

It can be hard to incorporate new ways of working when working within a team with other professionals. If the culture of the team is problem focused and adheres tightly to the medical model, as an individual practitioner it can be a struggle to start to do things slightly differently.

All I can do is encourage you to persevere. SFT is slowly increasing in its validity as a choice of treatment for a whole host of individuals. Wheeler (2005) found that solution focused practice related well to most legislative trends in the UK. In my experience more and more senior managers are starting to see that searching for solutions is an exciting addition to services.

Confines of my job

Some practitioners feel they would struggle to use these techniques because they wouldn't get the opportunity to apply them. They believe that in order to use SFT effectively they need to try to use as many of the tools presented in this book as possible. This is not the case. For me the elegance of SFT is that the techniques can be used as stand-alone interventions as well as in conjunction with each other. SFT is also more than just a set of tools and techniques; it is a change in the mindset of the practitioner from focusing on problems and deficits to looking for strengths and solutions. If all you manage to do is change your outlook on the individual you work with, the resulting conversations and discussion you have will lead to more solutions.

'I'm not a therapist'

Well that's good then, because what I've tried to do with this book is teach you techniques that are grounded in SFT, not teach you to be a therapist. Hopefully what this book does is add something to the competent skills you already have.

'I might cause harm by dabbling'

Compared with other therapies, there is a minimal chance of you causing any harm by using SFT. By taking the lead from the client, and seeing them as the expert on themselves and their life, there is little room for analysis and intervention by the therapist and what they feel might be best for the client. One of the key elements of SFT discussed earlier in this book is that the client is competent and has the skills and resources necessary to change. Very little harm can be done by encouraging clients to see their preferred future, exceptions to their problems and by offering compliments!

'I might get out of my depth'

Start slowly. It takes a great leap of faith to start using a new set of tools. Instead of jumping straight in with the Miracle Question (see Chapter 6), maybe begin with highlighting to the client times when their problem may not have been as prominent. Remember, if you do find yourself stuck, you can always return to the way that you were working previously. De Shazer and Dolan (2007) see your role as practitioner as leading from one step behind, expanding rather than limiting options for clients, and as refraining from making interpretations or assumptions about the meanings behind their needs, wants and behaviours. Armed with this, you'll be able to stay in your comfort zone.

'My clients might notice me doing something different'

I would hope so! Seriously though, it can be hard to switch from problems to solutions if you have been supporting someone for a long time. But it may be just what you need to start moving the client in a different direction. For long-term clients, discuss with them that you'd like to try something new that may help. In my experience clients often welcome the chance to be 'guinea pigs' and help you try out something new.

Quick tips for practitioners working in a solution focused way

Try to look at SFT as something you can incorporate into your practice and not as an alternative.
Always look for an ending. Approach each meeting as though it is the last one.
Ask the client what type of support they feel they need at this time.
Asking how the individual found doing a particular exercise or homework assignment is as important as the results.
Ask the right question at the right time. If you get an answer that surprises you, it's a good bet that that particular question wasn't asked at the right time.
Remember that you are a witness to the client's change, not part of it. Let them be the expert.
Ask 'What's been better?' rather than 'How are you?'
Lead by being one step behind – the client is the navigator, you are the driver.
Smile. Relax. Have some fun with it. Search with your clients for the most wonderful of solutions.
If what you're doing as a practitioner isn't working, stop doing it and do something different.

Building solutions

6

Non-problem talk

Many clients come to therapy drowning in their problems. Unable to see anything else about themselves but their problem, their conversation is saturated with problems. As long as the conversation stays stuck with the problem talk, clients will be unable to see solutions.

Sometimes referred to as 'problem-free talk', non-problem talk can be the first step in identifying solutions with the client. Although to the untrained eye these conversations can resemble simple small talk, the correct use of non-problem talk can do more than just put the client at ease and help build rapport. The simple chit-chat that occurs allows the practitioner to catch a glimpse at possible future solutions.

Non-problem talk is prevalent in the first meeting with the client, used as a way of getting to know the client and as a way to build rapport. However, unlike other counselling modalities, non-problem talk is encouraged at any time when the conversation gets stuck focusing on a problem. Box 6.1 highlights the benefits of non-problem talk.

Box 6.1 Non-problem talk

Creates a climate for change.

Connects with the person and not the problem.

Can be used at any appropriate time in the session.

Strengthens the relationship with the client.

Allows for self-disclosure by sharing some things you may have in common with the client.

Can be used to lighten a heavy-going session.

Limited self-disclosure can be invaluable in building the relationship with the client and in identifying solutions. Discussing with the client how you or other people you know or work with have found solutions can provide much needed inspiration to a client lost in their search to do 'something different' that may be the springboard to solutions.

Although this may seem as advice-giving, SFT stays true to the premise that the client is the expert by simply offering these insights into possible solutions as suggestions. The whole issue of advice-giving in SFT is adequately discussed in De Shazer and Dolan (2007), where Berg simply poses the question of why if – as a solution focused practitioner – you knew something that would help the client, you would not share that with them.

In the following example the therapist steers the conversation away from the presenting problem, creating a more solution focused atmosphere where the client can start to see something other than their problem.

Therapist: I can tell your anxiety is really causing you a lot of difficulty at the moment. But I've just realised, the only thing I know about you is how your anxiety is affecting you. Would you be happy to tell me something else about yourself? What did you like to do before this anxiety took over?

Client: It's hard to think there is anything but this terrible anxiety I feel. But I guess I really like to cook. But recently I've just been too anxious. And having no appetite I really have no motivation.

Therapist: Ahh ... you like to cook. What's your signature dish? What do you like to cook the most?

Client: Oh that would be lasagne. I love to cook it and to eat it!

Therapist: Really. Wow! I've always struggled to get that right. All those layers. I always leave the lasagne to my partner who seems to cook nothing else [*smiles*]. And are you any good at cooking? Does your family like your cooking?

Client: Sort of. Well, I think I am anyway! I haven't had any complaints yet. Except when I try to get my teenagers to eat salad!

Therapist: Ha ha! I can see that would be an ongoing struggle. And are you a 'follow the recipe to the letter' kind of person or do you like to make it up as you go along?

Client: Definitely a recipe person. I feel lost without one! But as I said, I just don't have any appetite at the moment.

Therapist: I understand that. Let's see if we can work together to do something about that.

Although the problem is always at the forefront of the client's mind, the therapist gradually gets to see a side of the client where the problem is not evident. The smiles and jokes create a dialogue more conducive to finding solutions. Although at this stage the client may be too problem focused to see that cooking could be an exception to their problem, the skilled practitioner saves this as a possible solution for later conversations.

De Shazer and Dolan emphasise the importance of non-problem talk:

> *Any solution has to fit into everyday life. Otherwise, it will, of course, be rejected. So we need some details of this everyday life. Here the client is the expert and his [sic] competence can be put to use in taking steps he already knows about to build a solution. Of course the problem is part of everyday life, but it is something the client wants to eliminate, so we want to construct things so that it becomes logical and reasonable for this competent person to do something.*
>
> (de Shazer and Dolan, 2007, p74)

Non-problem talk: example questions
I know very little about you apart from what brings you here today. What would you feel happy to tell me about yourself?
What are you interested in?
What do you enjoy doing? How about before the problem started?
What are you good at?
Tell me a little more about your family?
How would your best friend describe you?

The stance of not knowing

If someone asked me what it is I love about my mum or dad, my answer would be a unique, personal description if what it is that I see in them, how I perceive them, and how I experience our relationship. Although there may well be similarities and commonalities between how I would answer and how my sister would, fundamentally we would answer differently.

> **'If your mind is empty, it is always ready for anything; it is open to everything. In the beginner's mind there are many possibilities, but in the expert's there are few.'**
> *Shunryu Suzuki Quoted in Winokur (1989, p125)*

The same would be true if I was asked what it is that I love about my partner. How I see her and how I relate to her is different from how her friends and family do. None of us is wrong here – we simply all have different experiences of the same things.

This concept is fairly well recognised. In fact, when I first met my partner I was asked what it was that I found attractive about her; what was it about her that made me want to marry her. People were generally inquisitive and wanted to know more about what I saw. From my answer they learned more about me and more about her. Their natural inquisition taught them what it is I experience about my partner that they may not be aware of.

A major component of Solution Focused Therapy encourages the practitioner to take a stance of not knowing. The vast array of questions we ask is designed to find out what it is about something the client has shared with us that is important to them; what it is that makes a difference to them. The client is the expert on themselves, with the therapist being the expert on therapy and change management.

For example, many individuals who are depressed have come to sessions and told me that taking a walk on a bright sunny day makes them feel a little better. This is something I can relate to – walking on a sunny day makes me feel better. But my aim as a SF therapist is to elicit exactly what it is about taking a walk that makes the individual in front of me feel better.

Let's look at this in more detail.

Therapist: So you mentioned that taking a walk this week made you feel a little better about things. That sounds really positive. I'm curious, what was it exactly about taking that walk that led to an improvement in your mood?

Client: Well, you know, it was a sunny day. It was just good to be out.

Therapist: Sure, I can definitely relate to that. I try to get out for a walk when it's sunny as often as possible. But I was wondering if it was a little more than that for you?

Client: Umm ... I'd been thinking about what you had said last time we met, and that maybe I should try to experiment with doing something different to see if it would make me feel better. I'd woken up that day and was feeling pretty depressed but at least the sun was shining. So I thought to myself I would try to take a short walk to the local park. It was the middle of the day so it was pretty quiet in the park and I just sat and listened to the birds singing and kids playing in the park. A couple of people even said hello to me. I guess I didn't feel quite as isolated as I thought I was.

Therapist: Wow! I'm really starting to see how this walk has helped you to feel better. Not only was the sun out, but you managed to find the motivation to try something different and while you were out you started to feel a little more connected to people again. What else was good about it?

Client: I thought I would feel really awkward being by myself, but it was nowhere near as bad as I thought it was. In fact, there seemed to be many people by themselves.

From just this small example of dialogue, the building blocks of solutions are starting to emerge. By taking the stance of not knowing, I have learned the following about my client:

- Taking a walk on a sunny day makes them feel better.
- They feel better when they don't feel as isolated.
- They are concerned about looking like they are all alone but by observing their environment they learned that this may not be a problem after all.
- They find it easier to go out when it's a little quieter and not so many people are around.
- They have taken on board discussions from previous sessions and are engaged in trying something different.

And from this, the following solutions could be the way forward:

- Isolation – minimising the times my client feels isolated could lead to a reduction in depressive symptoms.
- Achievement – my client felt like they had done something different and hence accomplished something. Tasks that can give the client a sense of achievement may be well received.

- Crowds – Initially my client finds it hard to do something new in crowded situations. Initial solutions should focus on less crowded environments.
- Exercise – Simply going out and being active has helped my client feel better.

Therapist as the expert

My initial training in psychological therapy was with the therapist as expert – my training as a psychologist and counsellor put the emphasis on the all-knowing practitioner, guiding the client to make changes in their life in a way that the research and my training and experience indicated.

Taking the above example, I guess I would have taken what the client said at face value. After all, I am well aware of the research (see Biddle *et al*, 2000) and National Institute for Health and Clinical Excellence (NICE) guidelines on how exercise can lead to a lowering of depressive symptoms. And as part of my career I spent a couple of years developing the UK's first social relationships project for individuals with a mental health problem (see Proudlock and Hallé, 2006), so again, why would I question what I already know – reducing isolation can have a positive effect on mental health.

By communicating to the client that they are the expert on themself, I strengthen the relationship I have with them. By giving them the opportunity to verbalise what works for them, we have very different conversations. The end result will be that they will be more invested to try something different to help alleviate some of their problems.

Summary: the stance of not knowing
Adopt the stance of being like a toddler who is learning about the world – the endless 'why' questions that can drive parents to distraction. All the toddler is trying to do is learn about the world from our perspective. Take this same stance with your clients and reap the benefits in the form of a wealth of information.
Always keep in mind to question what it is about something that makes a difference to them.
Use what the client tells you as a basis for forming solutions and behavioural experiments that the client could try.
Never assume that just because you can relate to what the client is saying, your experience and meaning of it is the same as that of the client.

Compliments

Compliments play a big part in Solution Focused Therapy. They are used to genuinely express admiration to the client and as a way to reinforce the strengths, resources and solutions generated by the client. Used consistently and genuinely, compliments are a fundamental way in which we collaborate with the client to build solutions.

Let's start by turning to the dictionary:

> *Compliment: An expression of praise, admiration, or congratulation.*
>
> (The American Heritage Dictionary of the English Language, 2009)

As practitioners, we are not going out of our way to look for something to compliment our clients on. All we are doing is simply bringing to the forefront of our client's experience the personal qualities and strengths that may have been hidden beneath the problem. In the course of our conversations when the client identifies or shows us resilience, a sense of humour, evidence of hard work, compassion or any other quality that may enhance the solution we are working towards, we bring this to the client's attention.

De Jong and Berg (2002) identify three different types of compliments that are essential in Solution Focused Therapy: direct, indirect and self-compliments.

Direct compliments

Direct compliments are the simplest form of compliments and are expressions of praise and admiration by the practitioner in reaction to something the client has done or said. For example, if we were working with a client who had anxiety in social situations but had that week managed to go out with a friend for dinner, we could say:

Therapist: Wow, well done! You managed to go for dinner. From what you were telling me last week about how anxious you were getting that's really surprised me! How did you manage to find the confidence to go out?

Compliments can either stand alone as a positive evaluation, or they can be used to formulate the next question designed to explore just how the client managed to do what they did, as in the example above.

Indirect compliments

Indirect compliments tend to take the form of questions that express a desired outcome or state for the client. The above example contains both direct and indirect compliments. The initial praise for managing to go out for dinner is the direct compliment, with the question about confidence being the indirect compliment. The therapist compliments the client on having the confidence to go out. In doing so, the therapist enables a socially anxious client to realise that they must have had some confidence in order to actually venture out. This quality may have previously been hidden as the anxiety had started to take hold.

Indirect compliments can also be implied through a relationship that the client has with somebody who is close to them. The practitioner encourages the client to see a quality in themselves through the eyes of someone else, as the following examples show:

Therapist: If your best friend was here with us now, what might they say were some of your qualities that made you a good friend to them?

Therapist: What might your boss tell me that you were good at in your job?

Therapist: If your children were here, what might they tell me that they loved about their dad?

Through the answers generated from these indirect compliments, the client starts to identify exceptions to the problems they are enmeshed with. Indirect compliments are always preferable to direct compliments as clients start to generate their own strengths and resources, adding to their ability to build solutions.

Self-compliments

Probably the hardest and rarest forms of compliments are self-compliments. Clients may occasionally tell us about the positives they have experienced in their lives, such as finding the strength to come to therapy, or stopping a destructive form of coping with distress. Let's look at an example of a client who has managed not to self-harm for a couple of weeks:

Client: I don't quite know how I did it, but I've not cut myself now for over two weeks. Maybe it's because I've been coming here.

Therapist: Wow, that is good. You seem surprised that you've managed to do it. Has it been difficult for you to do?

Client: Very difficult. And it's not even been one of the goals we looked at. But when I decided to come for help I decided there and then that I needed to learn to cope better.

Therapist: That's good to hear. It shows great strength not only to stop self-harming but to come for help. Where is that strength coming from?

Using both indirect and direct compliments, your job as practitioner is to reinforce these self-compliments and positive statements and help the client realise the progress they are making.

Some clients will struggle with compliments – they don't want to appear big-headed. For other clients it can be such an alien process to hear positives about themselves that they cannot take it on board. All I can say is persevere. As a culture we don't give enough compliments to each other, are always quick to notice the negatives and rarely comment on the positives. Start breaking the pattern and let the compliments flow!

Goal setting

A large part of SFT uses goal setting as a way of maintaining solutions. Goals can come in many different formats – some goals direct us towards something we want, others evolve from being driven away from something we don't want. Solution focused therapy uses a mix of both – we pick an end point, a preferred future, and work towards that.

'Man is a goal-seeking animal. His life only has meaning if he is reaching out and striving for his goals.'
Aristotle

Take, for example, struggling young actors. Their preferred future is to be a successful actor. That is their goal. But the reality of the majority of actors is they audition for role after role and are unsuccessful. What is it about their goal that stops them from giving up? Auditions are seen as the process necessary to reach their goal of being a successful actor. Each knock-back provides them with something new they can work on so that next time they may be able to move closer to their goal.

It's important to help our clients realise that goals are adjustable. As we experience life, what is important to us can change. Our vision of our preferred future changes as we move along our journey. I initially saw myself working in Information Technology. Indeed, my first degree was in Economics and Computer Science. But part of my degree led me to research Human–Computer Interaction, opening me up to the world of Psychology, leading to a readjustment of my goals.

But goals can and should be a lot smaller than the major readjustment of a career. If your preferred future is to lose weight, a goal could be to limit chocolate bars to three per week. The actual goal is far less important than how important it is to you and how you can go about achieving it. Without goals, individuals lack direction in their lives, struggle to make any long-lasting changes, and can lack incentive to change.

The goal must be important to the client.

Any goals that the client chooses to work on must come from the client and something they want to work on. If it is a therapist goal or a goal someone else wants the client to work on, the probability of achieving that goal diminishes. Only when the client is fully invested in making changes towards their goal will the client start to do something different and start building solutions.

Keep goals small, achievable and realistic.

The most common error when it comes to goal setting is in having unrealistic expectations of what can be achieved. Once clients start to formulate their preferred future, they come up with the most elaborate goals for themselves, having unrealistic expectations of what they can achieve. Goals such as 'We'll never argue again', 'I'll feel happy every day' or 'I'll be the next Wimbledon champion' are all great goals to have but are not realistic and for most not achievable.

Your task as the therapist is to validate this preferred future and compliment the client for the passion they express in formulating goals to achieve it. At the same time, you should also be working with the client to break down these goals to smaller, more achievable steps which are realistic within the context of the client's life. If the goal appears too vast, the client will be de-motivated and will give up before any change can be seen. Smaller goals allow for more immediate success, fuelling motivation and opening up another set of smaller goals and solutions to the client.

Make goals concrete, specific and behavioural.

I've lost count of the number of times clients have told me that their goal is to 'be normal, to just live a normal life' or 'to no longer be depressed'. Although there is nothing wrong with these goals, they are such generic goals that it can be hard to work towards a solution. Follow-up questions encourage the client to express these goals in more behavioural terms. As SF practitioners we want to know what the client will be doing when they are living this normal life and are no longer depressed.

Goals should express the presence of something or a behaviour, rather than an absence.

When an individual is embroiled in their problem, their main wish is for that problem to stop, for it to disappear. Think about the last time you had a problem – all you wanted was to be rid of it. SFT encourages us to look at goals as doing something different, and hence the presence of 'something else' rather than stopping something. For example, for those clients who want to lose weight, rather than expressing the goal as 'stop eating all the junk food', a solution focused practitioner would gently enquire as to what they would be eating instead. To make the goal even more concrete, we would ask what the client would be doing once they had lost the desire weight.

Goals are expressed as beginnings rather than endings.

By the time clients seek help they are often stuck at trying to solve their problems. Rarely do we see someone who has thought of coming to see us as their first option. As a result they desperately want the solution to their difficulties given to them as soon as possible.

When we ask clients to tell us how they will know when their problems are solved they usually describe the finish line – how their life will look when everything is better. Effective goal setting with clients encourages them to look at what the first step might look like. This helps to break what can seem like an inordinate task into a more achievable set of tasks.

The client sees the goal as involving hard work.

Enabling the client to realise the need for hard work reinforces that the problem is a difficult one, which justifies the need for the client to seek professional assistance. Any solution that arises from the hard work they do will increase a client's self-esteem and self-belief.

Reminding a client of the hard work that needs to happen to find a solution emphasises to the client that the responsibility for change is with them and not the therapist. By having to work hard the client will value any solutions that generate from the goal and, more importantly, own the solution rather than giving credit to the practitioner.

Goal setting: frequently asked questions

What if the goal is to get more understanding of the problem?

Solution Focused Therapy doesn't ignore the problem. At times it is vital to simply listen as the client divulges the intricacies of their problem. Some people feel the only way they can move forward is to get a better understanding of what has happened. Simply go with the client's goal. By doing so the therapeutic relationship with be enhanced. Eventually the client will be ready to work on another goal.

What if the goal is harmful to the client?

Rarely do we encounter a situation whereby the goals that the client wants to work on are detrimental to their well-being (for example, a client with an eating disorder who wants to lose more weight). But when it does happen, remember the stance of not knowing. Gently enquire as to why that particular goal is helpful to the client at this time, working with the client to decipher what will be different when that goal is achieved. Use relational questions to enquire how people close to the client would react to such goals.

Equipped with this information, work with your client to see if these things can be achieved by working towards a more positive goal. However, it is key to remember that using SFT techniques does not remove your duty of care to keep your clients safe.

What if the client has no goals?

Despite our best attempts to elicit solutions and goals from our clients, at times we are faced with a client who simply cannot see a preferred future or any goals that they feel they want to work on that would improve their situation. They may have become so entrenched in their problem that they feel that any goals would be futile.

In these circumstances, you as the practitioner can use a variety of techniques to broaden the thinking of the client. Asking what their peers may be doing, what they may like to try, or what a significant other might like to see them doing, can sometimes help ignite their forward planning and thinking. It's important to return to the central philosophy and Steve De Shazer's (1985, p7) quote – 'All that is necessary is that the person involved in a troublesome situation does something different.'

It may also be helpful if we can play devil's advocate, and ask the client if they feel a goal could be to stay the same; for things to remain problematic. The majority of clients will state that is most certainly not a goal. Turning it around you have the foundations of a goal – for things to not stay the same. From here, start small and see what needs to be different for things to not stay the same.

What if the client's goals are unrealistic, or are dependent on others, such as getting that perfect job?

I've always wanted to be the next James Bond, be it either on screen or in real life. The lifestyle of a secret agent has always appealed to me. My love of 007 is probably inherited from my dad and due to the many trips to see James Bond with him. But nonetheless, it remains as a goal. But how would we deal with a client who expressed a seemingly unrealistic and unachievable goal?

In these circumstances, pay detailed attention to what it is about that particular job that is important to the client. Sometimes it's not the end result, the final benchmark that's important, but what achieving that goal will bring with it. If the goal ignites their passion, provides a sense of fulfilment, gives them a challenge or allows them to mix with other people, we as practitioners work with the client to broaden their goal by enquiring how else they could find those things. When a client can express what difference achieving a goal will make to them, together we can brainstorm alternative ways they could make that goal a reality.

Exercise: recognising the steps of goal setting

Believe it or not, we set ourselves goals all of the time. When was the last time having a shower or buying a pint of milk was on your list of goals that you needed to achieve? Because these are everyday, routine things, we stop seeing them as goals. But if we start breaking down what steps we take to reach these mundane goals, we can see the skills, strengths and resources we bring to the whole goal-setting process, and in return we learn how to build more solutions.

'It does not matter how slowly you go as long as you do not stop.'
Confucius

Start with the basics. Work with your clients to break down these everyday tasks that they do on auto pilot. Start small so the client gets the gist of how to set goals. For example, think of a time they bought something from a local shop or had a shower. Then, using the questions below as a guide, get them to note down more details about how they might have achieved this simple goal. In particular, pay attention to:

Achieving Simple Goals

What resources did they use?

What areas did they feel competent in?

How did they know they did a good job?

What measure did they use that told them they had achieved their goal?

What were – if any – the obstacles that arose when they started to work on the goal?

Did they need anyone to help them with the goal? What did the support look like?

When you have built up a portfolio of evidence with your client about how they have set and achieved the most basic of goals, start to explore other examples of when they've set and achieved their goals.

When the client feels they are an expert on goal setting, move on to the following exercise, working with your client to achieve a current goal and the steps they need to take to get there.

Exercise: goal setting

Write down a goal that you want to work on.

REMEMBER: Goals should be ...

- Something that's important to you.
- Specific.
- Realistic and achievable.
- Involve hard work!

Does the goal express the presence of something rather than the absence of something?

For example, 'I will stop self-harming' becomes 'I will deal with distress in a different way from self-harming.'

On a scale of 1 to 10, please rate how close you are to achieving this goal where 1 is far away, and 10 is 'I have achieved it'.

0 1 2 3 4 5 6 7 8 9 10

What is your first step in moving one step further up this scale?

What strengths and resources do you need to achieve this goal?

Who else is involved in helping you achieve this goal? How will they help?

What could some of the obstacles be that may get in the way of you achieving this goal? How could you tackle these?

The Miracle Question

'You want me to ask what!'

That was my honest reaction when I was first taught the Miracle Question. My internal dialogue was going, 'Well that's just ridiculous. I can't see myself asking that! It may work in America but I can't see the clients I see in England being receptive. They'll laugh at me. Here they are coming to see me in the depths of despair and I'm asking about miracles! Never.'

'Miracles happen everyday, change your perception of what a miracle is and you'll see them all around you.'
Jon Bon Jovi

But I did. I do. And it works.

So what is it?

The Miracle Question is a pivotal part of Solution Focused Therapy. At the start of each training workshop I ask trainees what they know about Solution Focused Therapy. Nearly every time someone will mention that Solution Focused Therapy has something to do with asking about miracles.

Indeed, the Miracle Question has become almost a trademark of SFT and is one of the most useful and creative starts to the process of eliciting a description of a *preferred future*. The standard components of the question are set out in Box 6.2. The Miracle Question goes something like this:

> Suppose that tonight while you are asleep, a miracle happens, and all the problems that brought you here today disappeared. As this miracle occurs while you are sleeping, you do not immediately know that it has happened. When you wake up, what will be the first small signs that you will notice that will tell you that the miracle has happened?

By asking the Miracle Question, the practitioner can gain valuable insight into how the client would like to see themselves if they were free of their problems. It gives us more than simply asking the client how they see their lives in a year's time, because many clients would see themselves still struggling to overcome their current problems.

The Miracle Question gives the client the permission to start to fantasise about an ideal future – a life without their problems. Cognitive Behavioural Therapy identifies a common thinking distortion as catastrophising where clients get stuck in a negative spiral of depressive thoughts. Rarely do we allow ourselves the opportunity to think how good our lives could be if we could just get over our current difficulties. The Miracle Question opens up that opportunity.

Box 6.2 Components of the Miracle Question

That a miracle has happened.

The miracle resolves the problem(s) or realises the goal(s).

The client is asleep so they do not know it happened.

The discovery step by step that something is different.

Responses to the Miracle Question

There doesn't seem to be a standard response to the Miracle Question from clients, and I guess that's why I tend to like it so much. Each response is as individual as the person in front of me – reminding me that the client really is the expert on themselves. Every answer allows me as the therapist to gain a little extra insight into the client and how they want to see themselves.

Generally, clients experience pleasant emotions when asked the Miracle Question and in thinking about their response. Try thinking about how you would answer it for a second ... personally it feels good to imagine a future without my current worries. Feeling slightly more positive in the session can enhance the client's experience of therapy, further strengthening the therapeutic relationship, as previously discussed earlier in this book. It can also lead to another exception (discussed later in this book) to their current concerns.

Common responses

Silence

For most people this really is a strange question, especially in a therapeutic environment, more so if they had come to the session imagining that they would only be talking about their problems. Simply give the client time to absorb the nature of the question. Usually clients start off slow but when given the opportunity can come up with new goals or ambitions.

'I don't know.'

In their book *More than Miracles*, de Shazer and Dolan (2007, p44) refer to 'I don't know' as the client saying 'Be quiet – I'm thinking.' For others it may mean that they don't feel ready to share what their preferred future may look like. If they have become so entrenched in their problems, imagining a life without them may not be readily accessible.

What I tend to find works is to counter with 'Why don't you take a guess? I promise not to hold you to it.' This acknowledges the client's 'stuckness', and gives further permission for them to really allow their imagination to run riot.

'I'd have won the lottery!'

This is a great answer. And a great thing to wish for. If I was to imagine a miracle happening overnight I think I too would like to see my bank accounts swell to an amount comfortable enough to end all financial concerns. But I'm also a realist and fully aware of the 1 in 14 million odds of actually winning the lottery.

This type of answer allows the practitioner to start to work with the client to formulate a more realistic preferred future. Clients too are aware of the probabilities of winning the lottery. One way of responding to this type of answer could be to emphasise what a great miracle it would be to win the lottery, and then to ask *how* winning the lottery would make a difference. Take the conversation below, where the therapist has just asked the Miracle Question:

Client: Winning the lottery. Yes. If a miracle had happened I think I would like to wake up to learn I had won the lottery. [*smiling*]

Therapist: [*also smiling*] Wow! Wouldn't that be good. A couple of million pounds and no financial worries for the foreseeable future. Or were you thinking of winning a rollover jackpot?! [*more smiles*] So holding that thought in mind, how would winning the lottery make a difference to you?

Client: Well, I'd give up work for a start. Miserable job full of miserable people. And that would allow me to spend more time with my family.

Therapist: Ah OK. So not being in your current job would make a difference to you. And spending time with your family ... what sort of things would you do?

Client: Well with all the money I had I'd be able to buy them stuff and take them places. I love seeing the joy on my kids' faces when they go somewhere new and have fun.

Therapist: Right. I'm really starting to get the picture now – doing stuff for your family really has a positive result for you.

From this, the Miracle Question has enabled me to recognise the first green shoots of a solution. The client has told me how miserable their job makes them feel, how much they get out of spending time with their family, and how much better they feel by being able to do things for their family. Winning the lottery may have a probability of 14 million to 1, but changing jobs or spending more time having fun with the family is something the client could achieve.

The return of a loved one

A common response from clients who have lost someone significant is that their miracle would involve someone returning. Responses such as 'My wife would be lying next to me' or 'He wouldn't have had the affair that ended our marriage' are just a few examples from clients trying to come to terms with a loss. And like the response about winning the lottery, they are all great responses to what clients might want from a miracle.

Similarly though, clients are very realistic that the loss cannot be undone. The majority of clients who I see trying to cope with a loss have already exhausted all means possible to reverse the loss. And like the dream of winning the lottery, the practitioner carries on in much the same way, exploring with the client what would be different for the client if their loved one was back:

Client: If the miracle had happened, I would wake up and my wife would be back here with me. It would be as if she had never died.

Therapist: I can tell you miss her a lot. And I can tell that would take away a lot of your problems. But I was hoping you could tell me what that would mean to you? What difference would it make?

Client: Well, to start with I would feel safe and secure again. I would be part of something, not on my own. I'd feel more comfortable to go out and see friends, knowing that I had her to come home to. Oh, and I'd laugh again. I haven't laughed for so long – I think I may have forgotten how to. I think I just feel isolated.

Therapist: She was very special to you. It can be hard to feel connected again when you lose someone so close. What else were you able to do when she was with you?

Finding solutions out of grief and loss is a hard process for both client and practitioner. The Miracle Question helps us to gauge how far a client has got with their grief. From the above example, some clients will be able to work with the practitioner to see that, by breaking the isolation, a small solution could be formed.

Others will be so full of grief that the Miracle Question has allowed them to share a little more of what their loved one meant to them. As a practitioner, allow the client to expand on what that loss means. Encourage them to tell you more about what their loved one meant to them, and what this person would want for the client today. Eventually, explore with the client how ready they may be for solution talk by asking, 'How will you know when it is time to stop grieving and start to do something, even the smallest thing, differently?'

The vanishing act response

Many clients will simply describe the absence of symptoms, for example, 'I won't feel anxious', 'I will no longer feel depressed' or 'A huge weight would have been lifted'. Although all great responses, SFT tries to get clients to express goals and preferred futures in positive terms.

To help clients develop more positive solutions, simply ask them what they might feel instead, and then ask what they might do differently when they start to feel this way:

Client: I guess when I wake I wouldn't be feeling anxious any longer.

Therapist: Wow, that would be great. From what you've been saying, the anxiety is really taking over your life. But if you weren't feeling anxious any more, what do you think you might be feeling instead?

Client: I'm not sure. Anxiety is all I've known for so long. Maybe a little more in control.

Therapist: Great! And if after this miracle had happened you were feeling a little more in control, what do you think I might see you doing differently?

De Shazer and Dolan (2007) encourage us to look at clients' responses as interrelated parts of 'feel, think and do'. When clients give a response about how they will feel differently, the practitioner needs to encourage the client to relate that to how they might 'do' something differently.

In a similar way, when we are told by the client that they will think differently about a situation, we follow up with how that will lead to them doing something differently. Solution Focused Therapy aims to get the client to see that by doing something differently they might be able to find more resources and hence solutions to their problems.

A preferred future

In the majority of cases, clients are able to respond with a clear picture of how their life would be. They are able to describe a vision of what they would be feeling, thinking and doing. It can be filled with a host of solutions, blending parts of how they were in the past before their problematic situation occurred, with hopes and dreams for a better future. Some of the exercises in the last part of this book are designed to magnify their imagination.

Expansions and alternatives

As long as the foundations of the Miracle Question are utilised (see above), then the practitioner is free to adapt the question in whatever way they feel is most applicable to the client in front of them. Sometimes I feel that asking about miracles per se is not right for a particular client at that particular time.

Occasionally the client will unwittingly invite you to ask the Miracle Question. For example, as part of my general assessment I enquire about the medication the client may be taking. Sometimes a client can respond with, 'I just wish there was a magic pill just to take this all away.'

Here's the opening you need to ask an alternative form of the Miracle Question. It begins with my emphasising with the client how wonderful such a 'magic pill' would be:

Therapist: That would be good – it would certainly put me out of work and many of my colleagues, but unfortunately we don't have such a pill. But let's imagine for a second if we did have one. Suppose there was such a pill that I could give you. And you go home tonight, have your dinner and then chill out in front of the TV, and after a couple of hours, you start to feel a little sleepy. But tonight, as well as taking all the medication you've already told me about, you take a magic pill that has been put into your medication by mistake. And what this pill does is take away all of the problems we've talked about so far. But because it's been put into your medication by mistake, you're unaware you've taken it. What do you think is the first thing you would notice that would be different tomorrow?

Similarly, clients have asked me if I have a magic wand. As above, just incorporate it into your question. Go with the opening. By using the client's language, not only will it increase the flow of the conversation, but clients may also be more open to the Miracle Question.

Setting the scene

More recently, and following from De Shazer and Dolan (2007), I've taken more time in asking the Miracle Question and start by setting the scene. In a similar way to guided imagery, I talk the clients through what they may do after the session finishes to the time when they go to sleep and the miracle happens. This is a great time to use what you have leaned so far about the client, incorporating it into your scene. Take the following:

Therapist: So after you leave here today, you go home and do what you normally do – pick the kids up from school, make some dinner, read them a bedtime story and then start to chill out, maybe watch a little TV, maybe those soap operas you mentioned earlier. Who knows! After a while, you begin to feel a little sleepy and take yourself off to bed. You read a little, before eventually dropping off to sleep – your bedroom is just right – not too hot, not too cold. Maybe you start to dream a little. And while you are enjoying a deep sleep, a miracle happens, and all the problems that brought you here today disappeared. As this miracle occurs while you are sleeping, you do not immediately know that it has happened. When you wake up, what will be the first small signs that you will notice that will tell you that the miracle has happened?

Although much longer to set up, painting a picture of having a normal, relaxing evening makes the miracle seem a little more real to clients – like it really could happen. Using the words and details the client gave you when previously asked the question increases the client's feelings of comfort and security. When relaxed and comfortable, clients tend to respond better to the Miracle Question.

When the Miracle Question seems too much ...

Occasionally, I just don't feel the client is ready to start exploring miracles. In these situations I start to ask what can only be described as a 'watered down' version, instead of encouraging the client to lose themselves in their imagination.

What the Miracle Question is trying to do is to discover the client's preferred future. Any question that can get the client to think forward to a time when their problems are minimised could open up solution talk. Take the following two examples:

Therapist: If I was sitting here with you in a years' time, and you were telling me about all the things you would have done to make yourself feel better, what would some of those things be?

Therapist: If I was to bump into you in a couple of years' time, and miraculously all your problems had disappeared, what would you be doing differently from now? What would I see about you that was different?

At other times the standard Miracle Question can be too broad, overwhelming the client. If you sense this is happening, try breaking the question down into smaller 'miracles' – instead of all problems disappearing, focus on one specific problem. For example, if the client has mentioned a general lack of confidence, the following may be useful:

Therapist: Let's pretend for a moment that I had a new type of medication that could give you this confidence we have been talking about today. If you could take this confidence pill, how would things be different? Who would notice the most that the pill was starting to work? Have there been any times when you've been able to do some of these great things even though you had yet to take the confidence pill?

In essence, all we are trying to do is find that preferred future. Once we have that and the goals the client wants, we can work, step by step, with our clients to do something different.

Now that I've got you believing in miracles

Once you've actually asked the question, explored the client's initial response and transferred thinking and feeling responses into what they are going to do differently, it's time to build on these foundations and expand on the miracle you've helped the client describe.

Changing the focus briefly away from the preferred future, questions such as 'Will you wake at the usual time?' and 'Will you know at once that the miracle has happened? How will you know? What will happen next?' allow the client to really think about how their life will be different if a miracle happens and takes away their problems. Gentle lines of enquiry help reinforce the possibility that there is a life outside the constraints of their problems.

'A miracle is an event which creates faith. That is the purpose and nature of miracles. Frauds deceive. An event which creates faith does not deceive: therefore it is not fraud, but a miracle.'
George Bernard Shaw (Quoted by Thinkexist.com)

Who else would see this change?

Once the client has exhausted all possible changes that this miracle might make, our next set of questions tries to determine who in the client's life might notice these changes.

Solution Focused Therapy is relational, that is, it tries to get the client to position themselves, their problems and solutions in the relationships they are intrinsically linked into.

The following questions all help the client to see the miracle through the eyes of someone else:

- What would your partner notice that was different about you the morning after the miracle? What might they see you doing differently? How would they tell this miracle had happened?
- What about your children – what would they notice?
- And the people from work – would you do anything different with them?
- What would I see you doing differently if this cloud of depression had left you?
- Who else?

Some clients may not have anyone in their lives who can express an opinion about what would be better. Depending on the client's situation, don't be afraid to bring in whoever or whatever you can. If they have a baby, ask what that baby might notice that was different. If they have a dog, discover what the dog might sense was different if this miracle happened. And if you're really stuck, try asking what they might see different when they look in the mirror the morning after the miracle has happened. You might be surprised at what you might hear.

But what about the real world ...

Once you feel the client has exhausted all possibilities resulting from this miracle, slowly bring the client back into their current world and explore whether any part of their miracle is already happening. Typically, a small part of the miracle is already occurring, but due to the tunnel vision provided by our client's problem, they have been unable to recognise it.

Therapist: Your miracle sounds really positive. I can really tell by the look on your face how good that life outside of your problem feels to you. Unfortunately I can't make a miracle happen for you. But I was wondering if any part of what you've described may already be happening some of the time?

Client: I guess I don't feel as anxious when I'm hanging out with my friends. Not all the time. But yeah, sometimes I feel the anxiety isn't on top of me so much.

Therapist:: Interesting. So when you're hanging out with your friends, you feel like you've escaped a little from the anxiety. What is it that you do with your friends that makes it feel a little bit like the miracle has happened?

Client: Mostly they just talk to me. Sometimes not even about my problems. They just treat me like a regular person.

Therapist: Not a 'regular person'! How dare they?! What kind of friends are they? [*smiles*] That really does sound like a miracle! Jokes aside though, do you think you could spend a little more time just hanging out with your friends and being a regular person?

If parts of the miracle aren't yet visible to the client, start exploring what the client may be able to do first to move closer to part of this miracle coming true. Find out how they could influence their lives right now to make part of this miracle happen. Together, discover the hidden resources the client has that can make the difference.

Most clients are only too aware that miracles don't happen, but by seeing if parts of their 'miracle' are already happening, the client can start to feel that there is hope and a way out from under their problems.

From the above conversation, we find out that the client's anxiety is lessened when they are hanging out with friends like a 'regular person'. And these mini-miracles are used to form the next integral part of SFT – exceptions.

Exercise: Miracle Question

A step-by-step guide to asking and expanding on the Miracle Question

1 **Preamble:** explain to the client you're going to ask them a bit of a strange question.

I was hoping I could ask you a little bit of an unusual question?

2 **Set the scene:** using guided imagery, set the scene for the client, getting them comfortable, ready to sleep, ready for the miracle!
Remember to use the client's language and the information they have already given you.

3 **The question:**
Suppose that tonight while you are asleep, a miracle happens, and all the problems that brought you here today disappeared. As this miracle occurs while you are sleeping, you do not immediately know that it has happened. When you wake up, what will be the first small signs that you will notice that will tell you that the miracle has happened?

4 **Client's response:**

Make a note of:
a) Changes in feelings

b) Changes in thoughts

c) What the client will be doing differently

5 **What else?**

6 **Who will notice that this miracle has happened?**
Ask specific questions using information gathered from earlier in the session. For example:

What will your husband notice that was different if this miracle happened?

7 **Who else?**
For example:

And your children. What would they notice?

8 **What difference will all this make?**

9 **Is any of this happening already – maybe a tiny bit?**

10 **What's the first thing you could do to move closer to parts of this miracle happening?**

How could you influence your life to make this miracle come true?

And then what?

Miracle Question: frequently asked questions

Does it really work – it sounds a little silly. Won't clients just laugh?

Yes, it really works. I've lost count of the number of times I've asked the Miracle Question, and nearly every time I get an answer I simply didn't see coming. Some clients struggle to find an answer – for many it was probably the last thing they thought they may be answering when they came to therapy. It can be quite an experience to see the change in facial expressions when the clients start thinking about a world without their problems.

And no, they won't laugh. Some may struggle with the concept, but it simply needs re-asking in a way that gels with the individual you have in front of you.

To use solution focused techniques do you always have to use the Miracle Question?

Absolutely not. The Miracle Question is only a small part of SFT and used to help the client envisage a preferred future. It simply allows for a more solution focused conversation.

When should I use it?

There is no hard-and-fast rule as to when to use it. Many solution focused therapists will use it in the assessment as it can provide a foundation for future work, but this is where you will draw on all your other great skills. It may not feel right to ask it in an initial session – a more pressing issue may have come to light, or you may simply want to establish a stronger therapeutic relationship.

I've generally used it as part of my assessment in the first session. But I've also used it months into therapy, when an opening occurs, when the session becomes stuck, and even at the end of therapy as a way of comparing a miracle at the end of therapy to the original miracle.

What if the client sees nothing?

This may happen – the client may be too entrenched in their problem to contemplate a different way of being. If it is the case, try re-phrasing the question or using any one of the other methods described in this book to elicit a preferred future. It may simply be a question of timing – maybe the client isn't ready to move on from their problem just yet.

What's the importance of asking what others would notice?

Solution focused is relational – it draws on the relationships the client already has as a vehicle for change. Asking what others would notice enables the client to begin to see themselves as others do. In a way they become an observer of themselves through the eyes of someone who knows them well.

De Shazer and Dolan highlight the importance of asking these questions:

> *Asking a question incorporating the view or reaction of someone with whom the client has a relationship anchors the therapeutic change more concretely in the client's real life, and provides a signpost of progress that she can look at in the future when she in fact does what she is describing and the other person responds.*
>
> (De Shazer and Dolan, 2007, p26)

Smith-Pickard re-iterates the importance of seeing ourselves through the eyes of someone else:

> *We live in a shared world where Laing says 'One recognises oneself in that old smile of recognition from that old friend'. Laing is pointing to the fact that it is through other people that we know who we are and it is also through us that they find a sense of identity. This provides us with a potent image for psychotherapy in the sense that it provides us with the opportunity to encounter ourselves differently, and vice versa.* (Smith-Pickard, 2009, p29)

Will the Miracle Question work for someone who isn't motivated?

It can be hard to know exactly what will work with someone who initially seems unmotivated to change. As a solution focused practitioner your job is to try to find out what it is that brought that person to see you and what their best hopes are for the time they are spending with you. What the Miracle Question can do is identify a goal the client may be motivated to work on.

Sharry (2007) looks at motivation from a social constructionism stance, stating that within this thinking motivation is not intrinsic or fixed within a client, but something that is constructed within a certain context and within certain relationships. With this in mind, it is important to remember that a client's motivation will change over time. SFT prefers not to label the client as unmotivated and to instead work with a client to create a context and relationship where they may be motivated to work on a specific goal. The Miracle Question could be the starting point of such a context.

A little note about 'What else?'

'What else?' is probably the question used most in SFT. It is a gentle way of enquiring if there is anything else the client can picture about their preferred future, exceptions, best hopes, goals or situation they are currently sharing with you. It shows to the client that we are listening to them as their story unfolds and reinforces to them that they are the expert. It helps us maintain our posture of not knowing.

'What else?' should always be used when using the Miracle Question as it helps us discover everything that may be better for the client once their miracle has happened. Keep using it until the client has nothing else. Take the lead from the client as to when it may be necessary to move the conversation on to the next line of enquiry.

Miracle Question flow chart

Figure 6.1 shows how the steps of the Miracle Question can be simplified into a flow chart. The first level shows some of the common responses to the Miracle Question: the 'Don't know' answer; a response of something unrealistic such as winning the lottery or the return of a loved one; the problem simply vanishing answer or the absence of the way they have been feeling ('I would no longer feel depressed') answer; and then a box for a positive view of how their future would look if the miracle had happened.

The chart follows each of these options and where you as the practitioner could go with the client to explore their preferred future – their miracle. As we move down the chart, we ask who else would notice this miracle, and eventually we see what they are doing already to make part of this miracle happen, or to elicit what the next step is to make part of it happen.

6

Figure 6.1 Miracle Question flow chart

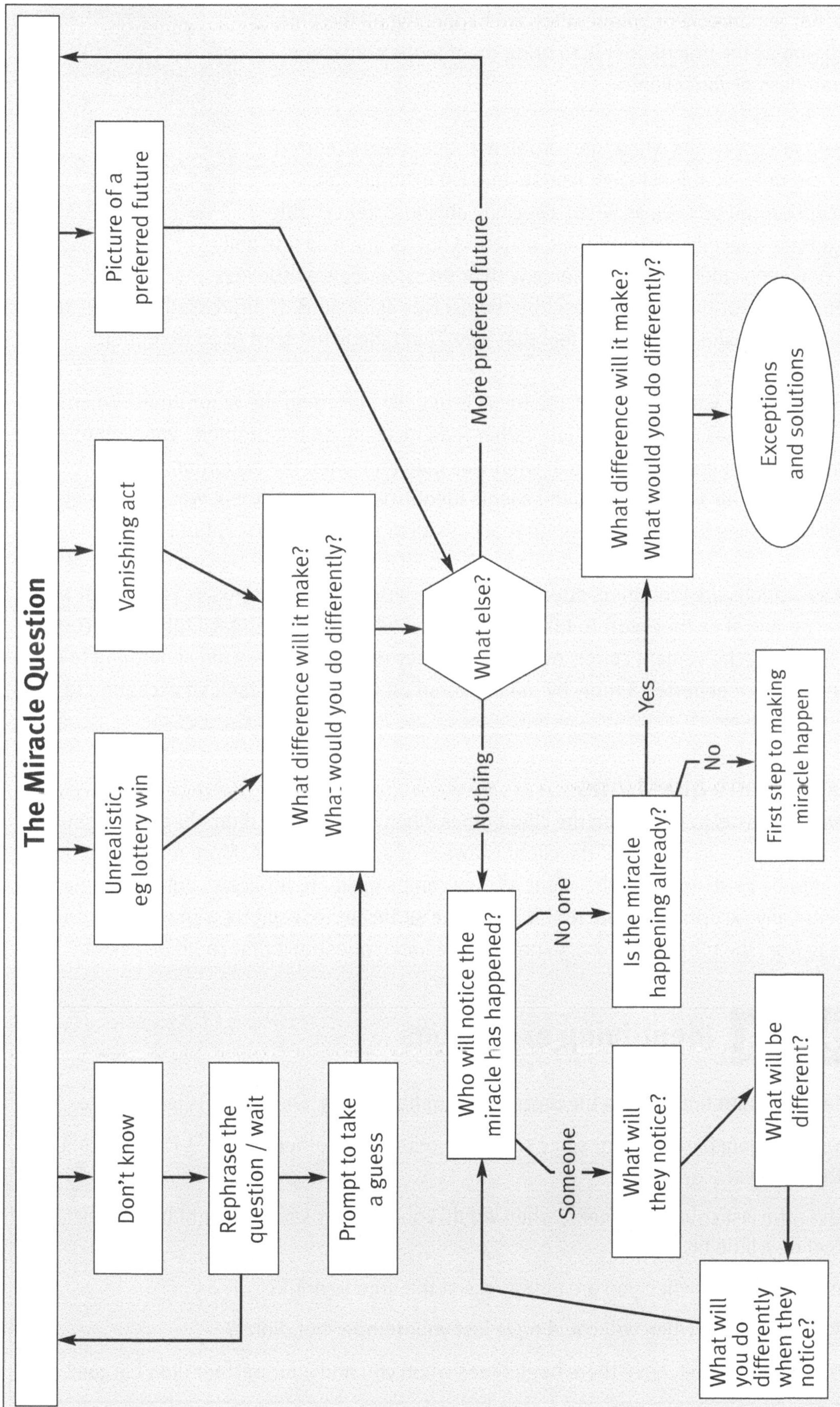

Exceptions

> **'Exception: anything excluded from or not conforming to a general rule or classification.'**
> *Collins English Dictionary*

Another major component of SFT is the use of exceptions. Exceptions are not remarkable or unique, they are happening all the time. Your job as the practitioner is to bring them to the conscious awareness of your clients.

There are occasions when their problems could have occurred but did not – or at least were less severe. For example, an exception can be seen as when a socially anxious client is able to attend a social event and their anxiety is not as much as it usually is, or when someone who presents with depression feels a little less depressed. For the client to describe themselves as anxious or depressed assumes they knew a time when they didn't feel that way. That time is the start of an exception.

When working with exceptions the focus is usually placed on the Who? What? When? and Where? of occasions of exception, rather than focusing on the problem. We want to elicit from the client intimate details of what was going on when the exceptions were happening. Our goal is to help the clients identify what was different when the exception was happening in order for them to replicate all or part of that exception.

As exceptions are identified, strengths are uncovered. The client lets us know what they are capable of as they start to take ownership of what they did to facilitate the exception. A sense of achievement comes over them as they realise that they did something to make themselves feel better. Simply by talking about an exception is itself an exception to some problems.

Exceptions questions

The first task is to elicit from the client times when the problem didn't happen or seemed a little better – to find out if the client is aware of any exceptions. More recent exceptions tend to be more useful to the client as they can be easier to replicate, but with some clients any exceptions to the problem may be sufficient to facilitate a change of focus away from the problem. Box 6.3 shows some initial questions that could be asked.

Box 6.3 Identifying exceptions

Tell me about times when the problem is not happening. Or when it is less severe.

You mentioned earlier that some times are better than others. What is it like during these times?

Over the last couple of weeks, when would your partner say you might have been feeling a little bit better?

Are there times when you are able to resist the urge to drink?

Are there times when you could have lost your temper but didn't?

Since we met last, have there been times when you and your partner didn't argue?

Once the client has found exceptions, our next task is to find out as much detail about these exceptions as possible, paying particular attention to how these exceptions were different from the problem times. The conversation should also focus on what the client did differently to make this exception happen – what was their influence on the situation? Box 6.4 highlights some of these questions.

Box 6.4 Doing the exceptions in detail

What was different about the time when the problem didn't happen?

Where were you when this exception happened? Were you by yourself or were there people around you?

How come this exception happened at this time and not others?

What were you able to do instead of not having another drink?

What was different about the times when you didn't argue? What did you do differently that could have made that happen?

What else is better at these times?

As with the Miracle Question, when we start to ask our clients about exceptions we also make our questions relational – we want the client to try to see themselves from the perspective of the people around them. Asking 'Who notices first when things are better for you? And then who? What is it they notice at these times? What else?' encourages the client to view themselves from a different angle, amplifying the exception and eliciting more details from the client about their resources.

Sometimes exceptions just appear. During the course of a conversation, clients will often let slip times when the problem does not occur or is a little less severe. For example, I often hear statements such as, 'I wish my son would go to school more like he did today', or 'I want to feel less depressed, like I was last year' and 'It was hard but I resisted the urge to drink yesterday'. In these situations, just go straight to the questions in Box 6.4 – start to do these exceptions in detail.

Random exceptions

Not only can clients find it hard to see any exceptions, but when they do they can be reluctant to take any ownership of them – they see the exception as happening independently of themselves. But some of the times the exception is purely random and nothing to do with the client. This is merely an opportunity to find out more of what the client did when the exception happened. The two examples below help to clarify what can be done with these random exceptions:

Therapist: So you felt a little better on Tuesday. What was different about that day?

Client: Nothing much. The sun was shining. That's about it.

Therapist: OK. That's good. Tell me what's different for you when the sun is shining? What is it that you do differently?

Client: Well everyone feels better when the sun is out, don't they? But I guess for me it makes me feel like I want to go out. That's what I did on Tuesday – went for a short walk.

Therapist: Ah OK. So the sun shining motivates you to go out. Do you think that it could be the getting out and walking that helps you to feel better as well as the sun shining?

Client: I never really thought of it like that. I guess.

The above example shows how we can turn a random occurrence such as the sun shining into a more concrete solution. The client above begins to see that feeling better may not be the full responsibility of the sun shining but may be in part down to their actions.

Therapist: So you and your partner didn't argue on Thursday. How did you manage to do that?

Client: I'm not sure really. To be honest I was a little surprised. I asked her to help me with the kids in the evening and instead of the usual 'It's your turn' she just helped. I guess it really was a miracle!

Therapist: It's starting to sound like one. There's nothing you had done earlier that day to suggest she may have been more receptive to helping you?

Client: Well, I had offered to help her with something she was doing with work but she had declined saying she wanted to do it herself.

Therapist: Ah, OK. So you offering your support to her may have allowed her to see your relationship as more of a partnership. Could that have been a possible reason for her help later on in the day?

Client: Maybe. I can see it may be worth offering her help again.

Therapist: I can't see it would do any harm. But tell me, how did you respond when she helped you and didn't argue like you usually do?

Client: Well, after I'd recovered from the shock I thanked her.

Therapist: Great. The more positive reinforcement you can give her the greater the chance this little miracle could happen again.

Once again a seemingly random exception can be reframed to allow the client to alter their perception to see that they may have had something to do with facilitating it in the first place. The example also shows how some 'random' exceptions can be encouraged to happen more often by acknowledging the positive exception.

From exceptions to solutions

Our last task with exceptions is to work with clients to see how they could increase the frequency of these exceptions or to see how they could fine-tune what they did to have a bigger positive effect. Simply enquiring as to whether the client can do more of what seems to be working can focus the client into owning their strengths and resources in problem solving. The exceptions they have described are successes they can own in solving their problems.

The dialogue below puts all of these elements together. The client has come to therapy for help with their anger:

Therapist: From what you've told me anger certainly seems to have a hold over your life. Not knowing when it might strike next is causing you a lot of distress. But I was wondering if there were any times when you could have got angry but didn't?

Client: No. I can't think of any times. I'm just angry all the time.

Therapist: Certainly. From what you've told me today I can see exactly why it can seem that way. But if I was to ask your best friend if there were any times when you didn't react to a situation, what do you think they might say?

Client: Wow – that's a tough question. Maybe when I'm at work. I don't seem to get angry as much when I'm at work.

Therapist: OK. So what's different for you at work that stops you getting angry?

Client: Well the first thing that comes to mind is that I can't – I'd lose my job if I did.

Therapist: Yep. I can see that. Anger in the workplace is generally not acceptable. What else is different?

Client: I think I generally feel more in control at work. And I think my colleagues respect me – I feel a valued member of the team.

Therapist: So when you feel in control, respected and valued you are more able to control your anger. OK. What else is different at work?

Client: Well, when a colleague or my boss says or does something that makes me feel angry, I can see that they didn't do it on purpose. You know what I mean? They are just trying to do their job.

Therapist: Yes, I know what you mean. You don't take it as personally as with other people.

Client: Yeah, that's it.

Therapist: That's great John. But I have to say, I'm a little confused. We started off at a point where you felt you had absolutely no control over your anger, but now it seems when you're at work, you have so much more control. Are there any skills that you use at work to control your anger that you could use outside of work?

In the above dialogue, the client has gone from seeing themselves as totally unable to control their anger to recognising times when the problem isn't so bad. On top of that, they have found the ingredients that enable them to be able to control their anger. From here the job of the practitioner is to amplify these resources and see where else the client can apply them.

Exception questions can be used on their own or in conjunction with some of the other tools mentioned in this book. Classically they have been used with the Miracle Question to see if there are any times currently when part of the miracle might be happening. Exception questions work well with the exercise 'Finding that positive lens', which encourages clients to highlight some of the small positive things that happen on a daily basis. As we will see in the next section, exception questions allow us to further expand on the solutions provided by using scaling questions.

Scaling

I like to introduce concepts by turning to a dictionary. Once I'd waded through the references to dentistry, weight, music and zoology, I found the following definitions that seem to aptly introduce the concept of scaling:

> a succession or progression of steps or degrees; graduated series; a standard of measurement or estimation; point of reference by which to gauge or rate
> (www.dictionary.com, 2009)

'There are very few human beings who receive the truth, complete and staggering, by instant illumination. Most of them acquire it fragment by fragment, on a small scale, by successive developments, cellularly, like a laborious mosaic.'
Anais Nin
(Quoted by Thinkexist.com)

The use of scaling is an invaluable tool for practitioners to use in Solution Focused Therapy. In its simplest form, scales encourage clients to put a numerical figure on where they are when describing a particular problem. As De Jong and Berg (2002, p108) state, 'Scaling is a useful technique for making complex aspects of a client's life more concrete and accessible to both practitioner and client.' For example:

Therapist: I can tell from what you've been saying that you're having a really bad time of it at the moment. Sometimes it helps to put a number on a problem. I was wondering if you could tell me on a scale of zero to ten how bad things are at the moment, where zero is the worst you could possibly imagine things getting, and with ten being the best outcome to this problem.

Client: That's really hard. I guess I would have to say a four.

Many clients find increased clarity when they are able to put a number on their problem. It allows them to channel their thoughts into defining the problem as it is now to the extent to which it could be worse and to how good things could be. In a way the problem for many clients becomes more real, more tangible and less arbitrary. With this increase in clarity about the nature of the problem, it's surprising how clients are more able to see solutions.

I'm genuinely surprised at the rating clients give themselves. They will express in great detail their problem situation and how they are not able to handle the level of distress the problem has caused them, and then when I ask a scaling question trying to determine how well they are coping, I'm expecting to hear a zero or a one and they come back with a three or a four. I feel it's important when using these techniques to express this surprise, and to find out why they haven't rated themselves at a zero or one. In this way we are expressing to our clients how impressed we are with their ability to cope. And from that we can see how to work with them to fine tune these coping skills and help move them up the scale.

Learning more about the client as the expert

Once the client has been able to put the number on the problem we can gently explore why the client has put that particular value on their problem. We can discover more about how they see their situation. Continuing from the above example:

Therapist: Wow! A four. I have to admit I'm a little surprised that it's so high. From what you've told me so far I was thinking it might be lower. Tell me what makes it a four on your scale?

Client: Ummm! I don't know really. I think a couple of weeks ago it would have been lower. But I've really been trying to not stay in bed all day and to talk to my friends a little more. I guess I'm not feeling quite as isolated as I was.

Therapist: OK. Good. So for you being a four means you are a little more active than you were and that you are maintaining your friendships. But I'm interested to know what a zero would look like on your scale?

Client: Oooh, I don't even want to think about that. That's a dark, horrible place where, no matter what I do, nothing makes a difference. That would be staying in bed and hiding away. Somewhere where everything bad and negative about myself would be staring me in the face.

Therapist: I see. That does sound a horrible place to be. So what would a ten be on your scale – have you a similar picture of how things would be at a ten?

Client: That's a much better place to be. I think I would back to being normal – back at work, enjoying my life, much more active. I would be dating again, spending more time with my friends and family and not thinking so negatively about myself. I'd be smiling again!

By simply asking the client to define their scale, we are able to learn so much about how the client thinks and what they want. Every time you ask them to define their scale, you will get a different answer. The client gives you the privilege of noticing how they think. And with this we continue our search for solutions.

From numbers to solutions

Once the client has taught us about their scale and how they see themselves now, we continue by asking our client to tell us what needs to happen to move them one place up the scale. Continuing with our example:

Therapist: So returning to where you are now, a four, what needs to happen for you to move one place up the scale towards ten? What could be the first thing you could do to move up to a five or even a six?

Client: That's a tough question. I don't know. I think to start going out a little more. As I said, I've started to feel better by not staying in bed. Maybe doing more of that could move me a little way up the scale.

Therapist: OK. By being up and about and going out more could be what helps you move up the scale. What else?

Client: Erm! Maybe I could start swimming again. I used to really like going to the pool. It would really relax me.

Therapist: That sounds like a great idea. From what you said earlier a ten would be being back to normal, so the more of the things you used to do I guess the closer you would be to being a ten. Great. What else?

With gentle prompting and appropriate compliments, clients begin to see what small changes they could make that would bring them closer to their goals. The answers from these questions make great material for homework assignments – clients are asked to go away between sessions and start to do some of the things they have highlighted that will move them up the scale.

Scaling as a crude assessment technique

Another great use of scaling is that it allows us as practitioners to gauge the progress of our clients. As the sessions progress, clients can indicate how much progress they are making and how much further work is needed to get them to a place they want to be. Most of the time the goal of therapy may not be to get clients to a ten, but to simply equip them with the skills necessary to start them on their ascent.

Therapist: So when you first came to see me you told me that you were a four on your scale out of ten on how bad things could be. Using that same scale, where zero is the worst things could possibly be and ten is the best you could see things, where would you put yourself today?

Client: I was thinking about this the other day. I would say that at the moment I'm at a seven, sometimes even an eight.

Therapist: Wow! As high as an eight. What's going on for you when things are an eight?

Client: Some days I just see things more positively. I'm going out nearly every day and have started back part-time in my job. I was really nervous about going back but my colleagues and boss have been really supportive.

Therapist: Things are really starting to work out for you. I can tell you've worked really hard to get up to a seven and an eight. Is a seven or an eight good enough for you, or can you see what you need to do to move further up your scale?

Asking clients to assess their progress in this manner allows us to see whether clients need to continue to see us. When clients are able to come to the realisation that they've come as far as they need to, there is a higher probability that the changes they have made will be more permanent.

Sometimes asking clients to think about how long the progression up their scale might take can further encourage forward thinking and future planning. As a practitioner we're not too concerned about how accurate this estimation is, more that the client is able to see that at some time in the future a positive change might occur. However, if the time frame is too far into the future, it is worth working with the client to break down the steps necessary to move up the scale into much smaller, pragmatic stages that can be reached in a shorter period of time.

Whose scale – clients versus practitioner

The nature and design of the scale is not important. As a therapist I tend to always start with a zero to ten scale, clearly defining what a zero would mean and what a ten would mean. But sometimes the reply I get can seem as if the client has mixed up the polar ends of the scale, reversing them. Instead of correcting the client, SFT encourages us to use whatever scale the client is using. The design of the scale is less important than what the client assigns to those numbers.

Some clients just don't like numbers; the thought of using them to describe how they are feeling produces a blank. Instead of viewing this as resistance, explore with the client how the idea of scaling can be adapted to suit them:

Therapist: I can tell from what you've been saying that you're having a really bad time of it at the moment. Sometimes it helps to put a number on a problem. I was wondering if you could tell me on a scale of zero to ten how bad things are at the moment, where zero is the worst you could possibly imagine things getting, and with ten being the best outcome to this problem.

Client: That's really difficult. I struggle to use numbers. It's just not how my brain works. Sorry.

Therapist: That's OK. Is there anything that you might be more comfortable with? Some of my clients can relate better to grades, you know, A to F. Or maybe even a U!

Any scale can be used – colours, brightness, money, football teams – anything. As long as it has meaning to the client and the client can explain what being at a certain level of their scale means to them, you as the practitioner simply listen and learn from the client.

Scaling questions

On a scale of zero to ten, where zero is the worst you've been feeling, and ten is the best, where would you put yourself today?

What is it that makes it an 'x' for you?

On your scale, what would a zero look like? What would a ten look like?

What could be the first thing you could do to move one point higher up the scale?

What is it that you are doing that keeps it at an 'x'?

On a scale of zero to ten, how committed are you to reaching your goals and making these changes we have been talking about? What do you think might get in the way? What would need to be different for you to be more committed?

What are you doing that stops it getting any lower?

How will you know you've moved as far up the scale as you need to go?

What have you done to move from where you were on your scale to where you are now?

On a scale of zero to ten, how confident are you about being able to make some of those small changes we've discussed? What do you think you need in order to move to an 'x+1' on your confidence scale?

How long do you think it might take you to move one point up your scale?

What will be different when you are one point higher up the scale? Who will notice this?

Where do you need to be on your scale in order to not have to come back and see me again?

Scaling the suicidal client

One particularly effective use of scaling is in supporting the individual who is expressing that they are not safe and are suicidal. Despite the intensity of emotions and thoughts that hit the client who is suicidal, it seems the majority welcome numbers to summarise how they are feeling. By allowing the client to tell us what the numbers mean to them, we as practitioners can gauge how close they are to acting on these very distressing thoughts:

Therapist: From what you've said I can tell you're experiencing overwhelming levels of distress and confusion. I also understand you need some help in order to keep yourself safe, and that you don't actually want to die but simply for this level of distress to go away. I was hoping you would be able to give me a better idea of how safe you are feeling right now. On a scale of zero to ten, where zero is that you feel completely safe and have no thoughts of suicide, and ten is you feel you have no choice but to follow through with your plans to harm yourself, where would you be right now?

Client: Urm! Right now? I feel pretty bad. Maybe as high as an eight. Sometimes even a nine.

Therapist: OK. Thank you. I know this is really tough to talk about but you're doing really well. I'm just wondering what happens that leads to you being a nine?

Client: Sometimes my thoughts just get too much. When I'm by myself I feel I start to realise just how bad my life is, how much of a failure I am and how no one cares for me.

Therapist: OK. And what would you see happening that would push it up to a ten? Again, a ten is when you feel you have no choice but to act on your thoughts.

Client: I don't know. I haven't really thought about it. All I know is that I don't know how long I can keep feeling like this. I just want it all to stop.

Therapist: Oh OK. So there's nothing that you think might happen, but if things remain this bad you could start to feel more like a ten. Has there been any time over the last couple of days when it's been a little lower than an eight, maybe a seven or a seven and a half?

Client: Yeah, yesterday. Helen called, my friend from university. We had a really long chat. She said she was really concerned about me. She sounded like she really cared.

Therapist: Helen sounds like a really good friend. Is there anything else that has happened over the last couple of days that has made things closer to a seven?

Gentle questioning of the client allows us to learn more about where the client is with their plans to harm themselves. Scaling questions allow us to find out what might happen that could lead the client to reach a point where they feel they have to act on their thoughts. And finally we discover what's been better for the client, what takes the edge off these very distressing thoughts and feelings.

Scaling questions can also be used with clients who have already attempted to take their own life. Practitioners can use the same questions to see what had happened that led to the client reaching a ten. In this way support can be put in place to prevent future attempts.

Another benefit of scaling is it allows the practitioner to effectively communicate with other professionals who may be involved with the client. Regardless of whether others in a multi-disciplinary team have had training in SFT, scaling is an easy concept that translates across disciplines.

Sharry *et al* (2002) provide a more in depth exploration of how SFT can be used in supporting individuals who are suicidal. They stress the benefits of using a strengths-based approach while warning of the dangers of using SFT alone, given its lack of emphasis on risk assessment. However, the authors point out how scaling questions can complement other forms of risk assessment to establish levels of client safety. They suggest the following questions as empowering to the client while allowing clear communication of the intentions of the client:

> *'On a scale of 1 to 10, how confident are you that you will be able to get through the weekend without attempting to harm yourself, where 1 means you feel you have no chance and 10 means you are totally confident? What makes you that confident? What needs to happen to make you more confident ... to move one point forward on the scale?'*
>
> *'Suppose over the weekend your mood drops two points on the scale, what will you do to ensure you get back on track? What would help to get you back up to 6 on the scale?'*
>
> (Sharry *et al*, 2002, p396)

Rather than focusing on the problem of suicidal ideation, the practitioner and client work together to establish what the client can do if they start to feel unsafe. Although scaling is not the answer in keeping clients safe, it does provide the practitioner with a valuable tool for working more collaboratively with the client.

What about breaks and feedback?

For those readers among you who have read previous books and articles on Solution Focused Therapy, you may have noticed the absence of a section on breaks and feedback. Previously SFT has been taught whereby the practitioner has a break away from the client towards the end of the session, consolidates what has been discussed and then returns to the client with feedback from the session and tasks the client may like to do between sessions.

This book will omit such a section for two reasons. Primarily this book is about incorporating tools from SFT into your everyday work and is not about teaching you how to conduct a session using SFT. Second, in my opinion, end of session breaks are neither necessary nor practical in the majority of situations. Even if I am using primarily SFT in a session, I have not yet felt that I needed to take a break.

I prefer to offer feedback and compliments as the conversation unfolds, believing that they then seem more genuine. Having to go away and think about them removes that spontaneity and may give the message that the feedback is forced. It could be argued that in doing so I am not paying full attention to what the client is saying. However, if the whole culture of the interview with the client is positive in its search for strengths and resources, all I am doing is reflecting back these positives.

Occasionally I may ask the client to bear with me for 30 seconds while I review my notes, but throughout the session I am keeping an eye out for possible exercises the client could look at between sessions – some of which have populated this book. The homework exercises generated in the session are individual to the client and fuelled by what the client has expressed. They range from encouraging the client to try something new that they feel may lessen the power of the problem, to simply doing more of what is already working.

When are breaks and feedback a good idea?

The origins of SFT stem from family therapy. In this type of therapy there is usually a team of therapists working with the family – usually a primary therapist working directly with the family and one or more other therapists observing the session either via video link or behind a mirror. In this situation, breaks and feedback are invaluable to the therapy process – returning to the clients with a list of observations, compliments and suggestions from a team of therapists can be very empowering for the clients.

Any other situation where there is more than one practitioner may warrant the use of a break in order for there to be a consistent approach to what needs to happen next. Unfortunately, in many situations having more than one practitioner can be a luxury. Both in the NHS and in private practice I rarely work with other professionals when seeing a client – the cost implications of having two therapists simply makes it unaffordable.

A great place for feedback can be in any assessment letter you are required to write. Today it has become common practice for the client to be copied into the initial assessment, discharge letter and any other correspondence between professionals. I have found these to be a great medium to express to the client the resources and strengths they possess (Proudlock, 2009). Although not directly addressed to the client, I feel it makes it more real when part of a letter to another professional.

Speciality applications

7

Solutions in the face of crisis

> **'Great emergencies and crises show us how much greater our vital resources are than we had supposed.'**
> *William James (1920)*

Individuals in crisis can test even the most seasoned practitioners. There is a pressure on us that we need to do *something* to keep the individual safe – to ease *their* crisis. As a result, there is a temptation to return to a problem-solving response, to dwell on the events that have led to the crisis and assess the depth of the crisis. By gathering this information *we* feel more confident to handle *their* crisis.

Gilliland and James (1993) see crisis not as defined by an event itself but as an individual's unique perception of, and response to, a situation. The aim of psychological therapy is to empower our clients to view their crisis in a different way, encouraging them to do something different in the way they respond. Solution Focused Therapy (SFT) helps clients to re-frame their crisis and re-discover their coping skills.

By maintaining a solution focused stance, practitioners can help clients discover what they would like to see differently once the crisis has passed. Improvements are made by gently coaxing out of the client how their life may be once the crisis has passed. Practitioners work with clients to build up a picture of the past resources they have used when previously faced with crisis. Although the current precipitators to the crisis may be new to the individual, the majority of clients have had to deal with some type of crisis situation before. SFT goes looking for these past coping skills.

Where do I begin?

When supporting individuals in crisis it is vital to devote a significant amount of time to the problems that have caused the crisis. Empathising with their perceptions of what has happened to them will communicate to the client that you are there to support them. Searching for solutions and resources too soon could alienate the client, prolonging their crisis and sense of isolation. Simply begin with 'How can I help?', and start discovering what it is about the situation which has led to an escalation in their distress.

Initial answers will be swamped with problem talk. This may be the first time the client has told someone about their plight. It may be that the majority of the first meeting will be taken up with simply listening. But while you are attending to the course of events that has led to the crisis, listen out for resources, strengths, resilience and how they have been coping until now.

What's been different?

As with clients who are not in crisis, it is important to discover what has been different from their initial phone call and actually coming in to see you. A client's perception of their crisis can rapidly change, and finding out these changes can help future solution building.

What have you tried?

When you feel the client has exhausted their description of their crisis, slowly engage the client in solution talk. It can be tough to know when to start building solutions, but a good rule of thumb is to wait until the client is offering no new information about their problem situation, that is, when they appear to be stuck as to how else to express their problem or caught in a problem-focused loop.

Equally important as discovering what has been different since the initial call and the first meeting is to gauge what has happened since the crisis began. In my experience, calling for help from a professional tends to be last on the list of strategies clients use to ease their distress. Asking how they have coped so far could uncover a barrage of coping strategies. Of these, some will show great resilience. Other coping strategies may need fine-tuning to assist the client onto a different course to deal with their crisis.

Start small

Empathically try to discover how the client has managed so far to endure their crisis and the pain they are in. Enquire as to how they have managed to get out of bed this morning and contact you. Ascertain what was different about this morning that helped them get out of bed. Explore past worse days when they haven't been able to get on with anything that resembles a 'normal' life. Determine how they've managed to survive long enough with their crisis to be talking to you now. Remind clients of how they have dealt in the past in times of crisis. Unearth how they've managed to cope so far.

Untangling the crisis to find solutions

Once you start to uncover these great coping skills, you as the practitioner should be back on track to use the tools already mentioned in this book. Begin by complimenting them on how they've managed to cope so far. In relating to the client as expert on themselves, explore how they managed to cope the way they did. Search for exceptions of times when the intensity of their situation seems to ease, and use scaling questions to gauge where they see their current coping ability.

Miracles and crisis

It's paramount to solution building to work with the client to get a picture of what their preferred future may be. This is no different when working with individuals in crisis. Asking clients what they would like to have different once the crisis has eased will convey to the client that they have some control over their future, despite the severity of their current situation.

But is the Miracle Question a good idea? Asked at an inappropriate time with a client in crisis it could damage any therapeutic relationship that has built up. Asked at an opportune moment it could give the client breathing space from their problem-saturated thoughts to start seeing a way out of their crisis.

There is no hard-and-fast rule in using the Miracle Question when supporting people in crisis. Every situation, person and crisis is different. My personal preference is not to use it, but to use other questions instead to explore how the client may view their situation if the crisis subsided a little.

Suicide and solutions

Clients who express suicidal ideation can trigger a multitude of thoughts and feelings in many practitioners. De Jong and Berg (2002, p227) discuss how the initial impulse on the part of most practitioners is to try to persuade clients that suicide is illogical, dangerous and hurtful to others, or to give an otherwise distorted response to the client's situation. Giving into this impulse, they state, 'may unwittingly exacerbate the risk of suicide as it is contradicting the client's perceptions and can further isolate the client'.

SFT techniques are still applicable in these circumstances despite the client's presentation of hopelessness and despair. A client who is still talking to you is safe and open to other ways of coping. You should focus on maintaining the client at this level and preventing them deteriorating further to a point where they want to act on these suicidal feelings.

Two particular aspects of SFT can be useful in these situations – exceptions and scaling. Exception questions can help us find out what is different about the times when the client does not feel suicidal. It is rare that a client will have suicidal thoughts 100 per cent of the time. Learning what is different about the times when the suicidal thoughts are more contained can be the building blocks for further solution talk and an increase in client well-being.

Scaling allows us to gauge just where the client may be in terms of acting on their suicidal thoughts.

Therapist: I was hoping you could try to give me a number about how you are feeling today. If you think back to yesterday when your friend first contacted us, could you tell me on a scale of zero to ten how probable it is that you would have ended your life? Where ten is 'I can't take this any more' and zero is 'I can handle this', where would you rate yourself?

Client: Ummm! I think I was at a nine or a ten.

Therapist: Ah, OK. Thanks for answering that. I know this is hard for you. So your friend was right to be concerned about you. You really couldn't take it any longer. And if you were to rate yourself today, using that same scale, has there been any change?

Client: I think so. Things don't seem as bad. Maybe a seven or an eight. I still can't see a way out of this, but I guess I'm not quite as ready to end everything compared to yesterday.

By using scaling, the practitioner has been able to determine where the client is now in terms of acting on their suicidal thoughts. Further questioning could be used to discover what has been better in the last day to bring that rating down to a seven or an eight. From those answers, the practitioner can see whether there is anything the client could do more of to bring the number down even lower.

Just as important as communicating this increase in coping skills is to elicit from the client what was going on that was making it a nine or a ten, and what they see might be the triggers that lead to it being a ten and them acting on their suicidal thoughts. A large part of risk management is to work with the client to find out what may lead to an exacerbation of their circumstances. Scaling questions help us to find these possible triggers.

Solutions are not for everyone

Despite our best efforts, some clients will remain at a high level of distress, overwhelmed by their crisis, unable to engage in solution building at this time. However, clients who have examined their coping skills, tried to see a preferred future and looked at exceptions are generally increasingly open to more intensive interventions such as hospitalisation or medication.

Solution focused techniques can be a great adjunct to practitioners working with clients who are suicidal and/or in crisis. However, as Sharry *et al* (2002, p398) advise, 'Given as yet the lack of empirical evidence for SFT with this client group, we must be cautious about abandoning traditional approaches to risk assessment and management.'

Summary: example questions

How can I help you today?

What did you do to prevent yourself from taking an overdose?

Are you surprised how you have responded to the crisis?

How effectively do you feel you have coped in the circumstances?

How would you have liked to have seen yourself handle the situation differently?

Suppose the crisis eases a little in the next week or so, what do you think you might see yourself doing?

On a scale of one to ten where ten means you are coping with your situation as well as you imagine anyone could, and one means you are not coping at all, how well would you say you are coping right now?

How did you get out of bed this morning and contact me today?

How have you survived long enough to be here?

How often do you have these thoughts?

How have you managed to cope for so long?

How come things are not worse?

What are you forgetting to do that has helped in the past?

What did you do last time that helped get you back on an even keel?

How do you think going to hospital will help you? How else could you get the same thing?

How come you've not tried to end your life already?

What has stopped you so far from taking the pills?

Solutions for relationships

Solution Focused Therapy is very adaptable when working with couples. The majority of couples know the reasons why their relationship might not be working, and often appear stuck as to how to move forward. There is usually little benefit to be gained by exploring the problem and assisting the couple in gaining further insight into their problematic relationship.

Relationship therapy is littered with solutions. Little effort is needed to engage the couple in finding exceptions – both past and present. At some time in the relationship there would have been more positive, fun times when the relationship felt strong. By focusing the couple on these times, solutions for the present and future can be found.

Questions centred on identifying a preferred future can also reap ample rewards.

Occasionally you might strike gold and uncover very similar preferred futures.

Realistically, however, the futures will be different. But from these differences the individuals learn to see what it is that their partner wants from the relationship. From this, the individuals can start working as a team to make a jointly preferred future for their relationship.

Scaling can also be a fantastic resource to the practitioner working with a couple. Together the couple can learn from one another what needs to be different to move one point up the scale to achieve the goal of having a positive relationship (or any other goal the clients want to work on). They may not agree with what their partner says, but hearing their partner talk in a positive way about improving the relationship allows for more open communication and ultimately facilitates solutions.

The relationship as the client

When I embark on relationship work with clients I tell the clients that the relationship is my client, and that our work will focus on making this client stronger and more resilient. Basically, I am in the corner for the relationship!

By doing this, and incorporating the SFT stance of not knowing, I can elicit from the couple how their actions affect my client, the relationship. As the sessions progress, when one of the individuals does something that benefits the relationship, it seems natural to offer compliments into sessions, enhancing the strength of the therapeutic relationship while emphasising these positive changes.

The exercises that follow highlight this notion of the relationship as the client. The first one can be very empowering for the couple and looks at the relationship as a balloon, encouraging the individuals in the relationship to note down what they do to inflate and deflate this balloon.

The second exercise gets the couple to highlight what resources they have that can support their relationship. Based on Murray and Murray's (2004) innovative Couples Resource Map, the exercise is designed to elicit from the couple resources they have that can help them tackle problems and obstacles within their relationship. Initially done individually, once back with the practitioner the work focuses on developing a shared resource pool that the relationship can draw on.

Example questions when working with couples

What would your partner see you doing differently if you felt more secure in the relationship?

How confident, on a scale of zero to ten, do you feel able to maintain these changes you have started to make in your relationship?

On a scale of zero to ten, where zero is 'I can't take this relationship any longer', and ten is 'this relationship couldn't get any better', where would you put yourself today?

If a miracle was to happen and take away all these problems you have been experiencing in your relationship, what would you notice that might be different about your relationship?

What's different for you when your partner makes you smile?

What's going on for you both when you don't argue?

How would you know you were able to trust your wife again?

How come you were able to kiss and cuddle your husband on that occasion? What was different for you?

Relationship balloon

Think about the last time you had to blow up a balloon – the effort you had to put in to get it just right. And then think back to how easy it was to let all the air out (usually when trying to tie that blasted knot!). To me it always seemed unfair that the air would escape in a fraction of the time it took to blow the thing up.

When I work with couples I tend to always ask them to think about their relationship as a balloon. Over the course of an average week they will do things that will inflate the relationship balloon, making the relationship stronger and more enjoyable, and they will also do things that will deflate that balloon, leaving the relationship flat and no fun to be in.

Most of the time the couples are unaware of what they might be doing to inflate or deflate the relationship. What one person may consider to be something that inflates it, the other person may feel is something which deflates it. For example, I might think that if I help my partner out with a piece of work she needs to get done by doing part of that work, I am being helpful to her. However, she might see it as me taking over and not having the belief in her that she can do it herself. What started off as good intentions on my part to 'inflate' the balloon has in fact led to it being 'deflated'.

The benefits of this exercise are multiple. First of all, by getting individuals to rate what they think they do to inflate and deflate the relationship helps them realise what it is they can do more of to make the relationship stronger. At the same time, by rating their partner, the exercise encourages more open communication allowing the couple to realise what works for the relationship and what doesn't. Simply making the other person aware that what they are doing may be perceived as damaging to the relationship can result in significant changes in behaviour. Rarely do couples who are malicious towards each other come voluntarily for therapy. Likewise, it can be a revelation for an individual to learn that some small things they do make all the difference for their partner.

Balloons are not just for relationships

This exercise can easily be expanded for working with any individual who needs to monitor their behaviour. When working with school students, for example, who need to work more consistently on their studies and behaviour, teachers can ask them to monitor themselves to see if they have inflated or deflated their academic record. The same technique can be used for employees.

For individuals who struggle with their mental health on a regular basis, I've adapted this exercise to help clients observe the relationship they have with their mental health. Most clients know that there are some things that they do that can make their mental health worse, and some they can do that will make it better. Using the analogy of a balloon, clients are encouraged to ask themselves, 'What have I done today to improve my mental health?' and 'What have I done to make things worse?' Over time, both you as the practitioner and the client will be able to get a better picture of what the client can do to better manage their mental health.

From balloons to solutions

This exercise relates perfectly to the central philosophy of Solution Focused Therapy. Once you have worked with your client to identify what inflates the balloon, that is, what is working, we encourage them to do more of it. And if there is something that is not working we get them to stop it and do something different. As the work with the couple goes on, the channels of communication are opened and they become more attuned to what each other appreciates and what each finds hurtful.

Exercise: relationship balloon

I want you to start thinking of your relationship like a balloon.

Over the next week, start to make a note of what you feel you do in the relationship that makes the relationship stronger: what is it that you do that inflates this balloon? Likewise, also make a note of what you think you do that might deflate this balloon. Also note down what your partner does that either inflates or deflates this balloon. Bring both sets of observations with you to our next session.

What do I do to inflate the relationship balloon?

What do I do to deflate the relationship balloon?

What do I feel my partner does to inflate the relationship balloon?

What do I feel my partner does to deflate the relationship balloon?

Exercise: couples' resource pool

When couples are tangled up in a web of problems, they can become ill-equipped to see the resources around them that can help keep their relationship strong.

This exercise encourages couples to pay more attention to these resources in three different areas: resources within their immediate environment, resources within the relationship itself, and resources within each individual.

Environmental resources: please rate the strength of the resource

0	1	2	3	4	5	6	7	8	9	10

0	1	2	3	4	5	6	7	8	9	10

0	1	2	3	4	5	6	7	8	9	10

0	1	2	3	4	5	6	7	8	9	10

0	1	2	3	4	5	6	7	8	9	10

0	1	2	3	4	5	6	7	8	9	10

Resources within the relationship: please rate the strength of the resource

0	1	2	3	4	5	6	7	8	9	10

0	1	2	3	4	5	6	7	8	9	10

0	1	2	3	4	5	6	7	8	9	10

0	1	2	3	4	5	6	7	8	9	10

0	1	2	3	4	5	6	7	8	9	10

0	1	2	3	4	5	6	7	8	9	10

0	1	2	3	4	5	6	7	8	9	10

0	1	2	3	4	5	6	7	8	9	10

Resources within yourself: please rate the strength of the resource

0	1	2	3	4	5	6	7	8	9	10

0	1	2	3	4	5	6	7	8	9	10

0	1	2	3	4	5	6	7	8	9	10

0	1	2	3	4	5	6	7	8	9	10

0	1	2	3	4	5	6	7	8	9	10

0	1	2	3	4	5	6	7	8	9	10

Couples are encouraged in the first instance to rate the separate areas individually. The following session is then spent comparing the ratings, developing a pool of resources the couple can draw on together with a list of areas which may need to be addressed either individually or as a couple.

Solutions in the face of anger

Anger is a normal, healthy emotion. Like other emotions, it's not something that can be easily controlled – we can't simply turn it off because we don't like it. It is a necessary part of our makeup, which can give us a vital boost of physical and emotional energy when we need it most. Too much anger, however, can have a significant impact on our lives, wreaking havoc on our relationships. Intense anger can lead to aggressive and violent outbursts resulting in a different set of consequences.

'Anyone can become angry – that is easy, but to be angry with the right person at the right time, and for the right purpose and in the right way – that is not within everyone's power and that is not easy.'
Aristotle

Unfortunately, over the years anger has received some bad press. Modern society views anger in a negative way and as an inappropriate response to frustration. We're told that we need to be calm and assertive and 'deal' with our anger in an appropriate way. 'Anger Management' has been the buzz term over the last ten years, with the bookshelves filled with anger management tools and techniques. Anger = Bad.

'When angry, count to four. When very angry, swear.'
Mark Twain

I've always felt the term 'Anger Management' to be misleading. It implies we can control an emotion which by its very nature is uncontrollable. Instead, what we want as a society is 'Aggression Management'. For some it may not be a case of stopping anger, but learning what to do with these angry feelings when they occur – or as Aristotle put it, learning to notice anger at the appropriate time.

Anger and Solution Focused Therapy

Solution Focused Therapy can be very effective in helping clients gain more control over their anger. Many clients who come to therapy for help with anger perceive their anger as an instantaneous phenomenon over which they are powerless to exercise any control. They see themselves as being calm one moment and explosive the next.

The aim of SFT when faced with a client trying to deal with their anger is twofold: empower the client to pay more attention to their anger and thus communicate a sense of greater control over their anger; and work with the client to develop a pool of tools and resources they can use to effectively deal with their anger when it gets to danger levels.

Anger solutions step by step

The full catalogue of solution focused tools and techniques can be used in helping a client deal more effectively with their anger. Treating the client as an expert on their anger is a vital first step. Exploring their anger in detail enables both the client and you as the practitioner to learn more about the How? When? Where? What? and Why? of the anger. I know how it feels when I get angry but anger is intimately personal to every individual. Only by exploring the client's experience can we start to find solutions to their anger.

Once we have a clearer picture of their anger, use exception questions to find out when the client doesn't get angry or when it happens less intensively. Paying more attention to times when the client could have got angry but managed to remain calm, allows the client to gain confidence in their ability to control their anger. Exploring what is different at these times will add to the pool of resources the client has in dealing with their anger.

Scaling provides the client with a sliding scale on which to rate their anger. Instead of seeing it in all or nothing terms, calm or explosive, clients learn that their anger has many incremental stages. Recognising these earlier stages and utilising tools and skills from their resource pool to intervene at these stages can have a significant influence on how they manage their anger.

Working with your client to see how their lives will be different once they have more control over their anger gives the therapy a goal to work towards. Using the *Miracle Question* and other questions to elicit a preferred future can enable the client to see how they would like to deal with their feelings of anger and frustration. Examining how others around them deal with similar feelings can result in useful additions to their pool of resources.

Finally, when the client returns with descriptions of how well they've been managing their anger, use *compliments* and the *stance of not knowing* to reiterate how well the client is controlling their anger. Enquire as to who is noticing their calmer persona and reduction in angry outbursts, and the difference it is having on their lives. Discover if there is any further work to be done.

The following worksheet will enable you as a practitioner to help make the client more aware of their anger and the resources available to them to help conquer their angry outbursts. It can be used at any stage of your work with a client. Ideally, go through the sheet with your client, eliciting from them as many details about their anger as possible. Sometimes it can be helpful to ask the client to take the worksheet home and fill it out after an angry incident with the people most affected by their anger in order to get a different perspective on their behaviour and how it affects others.

Exercise: finding solutions in the face of anger

On a scale of zero to ten where would you put yourself on an average day, where zero is perfectly calm, and ten is explosive anger?

0	1	2	3	4	5	6	7	8	9	10

Thinking back to the last time you got angry:

Where would you put yourself on the above scale?

0	1	2	3	4	5	6	7	8	9	10

What was going on for you when you were one point lower down on that scale?

What were some of the first things you noticed as you moved up your scale? Think back to anything you felt in your body, any thoughts you had, anything someone said, and so on.

If the anger helped you in any way, how could you achieve those same things without having an angry outburst?

Have there been similar times when the same sort of events have occurred but you haven't got angry?

How have you dealt with your anger on previous occasions?

How do other people around you deal with their feelings of anger and frustration?

In the future, how would you like to see yourself dealing with your anger?

Are there currently any occasions when you are able to manage your anger in a way you've just described?

When you are able to deal with your anger more effectively, what will be different in your life? Who will notice the most?

Next time your anger reaches a seven or an eight on your scale, what are some of the tools you could use to bring it back down one or two points?

Finding solutions at the bottom of the glass: using solution focused techniques with the problem drinker

Solution Focused Therapy is widely used in the treatment of alcohol and substance abusers. Solution focused questions amplify the times when the problem behaviour could have happened but did not, that is, when the alcoholic didn't have a drink. Unlike other approaches in dealing with addictions, the aim is not always for complete abstinence. Instead, SFT treats the client as the expert and allows them to determine the goal of treatment. As a result, the aim of therapy may be to give the client more control over their addiction and to achieve a higher level of everyday functioning.

Rarely do alcoholics come to treatment willingly. Like individuals in crisis, therapy is not usually top in the list of interventions that an individual considers when trying to get their drinking under control. We find that the impetus comes from partners, families, health professionals and employers, and can sometimes be linked to ultimatums. As a result, clients may be reluctant to enter into solution building.

Searching for exceptions to their addiction

Exception-based questions can be a powerful resource when working with the alcoholic. These focus on times when the individual could have drank but was able not to – times when there was evidence that the client could control their drinking. Berg and Reuss (1998) identify two types of exceptions – one created by the client doing something purposefully different and the other as just happening when the problem doesn't seem bad.

Once we have identified the first type of exception, amplify the Who? What? When? Where? and How? When engulfed in a problem situation, clients struggle to see that solutions are happening all the time. Exception questions capitalise on past successes; of times when their drinking did feel more controlled or didn't have such an impact on their lives.

Armed with these exceptions, clients begin to see a preferred future; a future of how they would like to see their lives if they could abstain from drinking or have more control over their drinking. Using the Miracle Question gives increased clarity to this preferred future and allows us as practitioners to work with the client to set some achievable goals.

What about relapse?

It is the rare client who goes in a straight line from being embroiled in problem drinking behaviour to abstinence or control. When relapses do happen, clients feel defeated and demoralised. When they return to therapy, they are once again filled with problem talk. All you can do as a practitioner is respectfully listen to their failures and accept and normalise their disappointment.

Berg and Reuss (1998) believe that clients return to treatment after they have stopped drinking again, not during their relapse. They see relapse as a normal learning experience – for a relapse to have happened there must have been success. They feel that after a relapse it is more beneficial to the client to focus on what led to them stopping drinking again and not on what led to them having the relapse.

After a relapse, our main intervention is again to search for exceptions and success. Find out details of how the client stayed sober before the relapse and how the client is staying sober now. Refocus their attention to their preferred future. Where necessary, renegotiate goals.

Useful questions when working with the problem drinker

What was different about when you went out on Tuesday that enabled you to not get drunk?

Let's imagine for a moment that you are able to control your drinking again. What do you think would be different about your life?

Tell me about the times when you have had more control over your drinking?

It's a big step wanting to stop drinking. What tells you that now is a good time to try?

Who would be the first to notice you had more control over your drinking? How would that be important to you?

What happened just before the relapse ended – how did you know it was time to stop drinking again? What was telling you it was time to stop drinking again?

What is different in this relapse and staying sober compared to other times?

On a scale of one to ten, where one is no confidence and ten is as much confidence as you imagine you could have, how confident do you feel that over the next week you could stick to your target of five drinks? What would need to happen for you to be one point further up that scale?

Who else could help you control your drinking a little more?

If one stands for 'I currently have no control over my drinking' and ten stands for 'I am fully in control of my drinking', where would you put yourself today? What would you need to do to move one point up that scale?

What do you think you will do when you get the urge to drink again?

It's not just about drinking ...

Much of the methodology and many of the questions can be easily adapted to work on most problematic behaviour. Clients requesting help with an addiction respond well to searching for exceptions – gambling, substance abuse, internet porn and overeating are just a small selection of how solution focused tools can help individuals gain more control over their problematic behaviour in a relatively short period of time.

Finding out how the client has managed to refrain from a form of disruptive behaviour is the obvious starting point in empowering clients to see that they do have some control over their behaviour. When working with individuals who deliberately self-harm, I simply ask what is different about the times when they feel distressed but don't self-harm. Similarly, with individuals plagued with panic attacks, ascertaining what was different about a particular situation that prevented them from having a panic attack gives insights into possible solutions.

Exercises to discover solutions

Foundations of solution building

So where do we start. How do we help our clients start looking at solutions rather than problems?

The following two exercises have become the foundation of my clinical work and are probably the ones I use most frequently as homework exercises for clients between the first couple of sessions. The answers to these provide the initial foundations for solutions, regardless of the presenting problem.

What I learn from these can help determine the speed at which I can work with the individual, as well as giving me the information I need to determine the first steps to meeting the central philosophy of Solution Focused Therapy (SFT) – if it's not broke, don't try to fix it; and if something is working, do more of it.

The first exercise asks the client to notice what happens between sessions that makes them feel a little bit better. Even the individual who struggles to tell you anything positive about their lives in the session is not depressed 24 hours a day, 7 days a week. Something will have happened that has made them feel slightly better than at other times. This is what we are looking for. Anything that alleviates what they are experiencing – even if it is only for a very short time.

When the client returns, really explore the table below with them to see what works for that individual client – take the stance of not knowing as described previously in this book. As a practitioner, you are trying to highlight the times when the client did something that resulted in them feeling better. The next stage is to get the client to do more of what is working.

The second exercise asks the client to list the activities that they like doing or used to like doing, and also to consider what it is they might like to do when they start to feel better. This has a couple of main functions. First, we get to learn more about the client – we can start to see the client as more than just a person with a set of problems. It equips us with the basics to engage in non-problem talk, not just now but in future meetings. Second, it provides us as the practitioner with a neat set of ideas we can encourage the client to do as a way of building small solutions.

Clients tend to like these exercises. They are a gentle introduction to SFT. The second exercise can be a useful comparison for the client to see what they used to like doing as compared to what they do now. It also starts to give them ideas about new things they might like to try – the first step to doing something differently.

Exercise example: what's been better?

Between now and when we meet again, all I want you to do is to notice what's different when you feel slightly better. Just notice what's going on when the problems you have told me about today seem a little better. What's different that is making things a little better? Remember, we're not looking for times when the problem totally disappears, just times when it seems a little easier.

Date/Time	What's been different? What were you doing? How did it make you feel?
28 August 0700–2030	Went for an evening walk by the river with my pregnant friend. It made me feel happy being outside in the fresh air with a friend who is very excited about having a baby.
30 August 1300–1400	Went for a long walk by the beach with an old colleague and stopped off at a pub for drinks. I gave her a birthday present and I was really excited that she liked what I had got for her. It felt good and healthy to be by the coast on a hot, sunny day.
31 August 1230–1500	Went to a market with my mum. It was a hot day and she really enjoyed herself. We had coffee, went to the shops and I sat in her garden. I felt happy my mum was having fun and I felt quite calm.
1 September 0845–0945	This was the first time I had done an hour on the exercise bike for ages! Felt good doing something healthy, listening to music – felt a bit like my 'old' self. A new month – a new start!
2 September 1730–1830	Had a happy hour showing my mum three dresses I had purchased for my friend's wedding. She got all excited choosing her favourite one and I was happy she was getting enthusiastic.
3 September 0900–1130	One hour on the exercise bike. Then put my new vacuum cleaner together and gave my flat a spring clean – felt good being active and practical instead of just sitting down studying.

The more differences you can bring back to the next session the sooner we can start finding solutions that will make a difference to you!

Exercise: what's been better?

Between now and when we meet again, all I want you to do is notice what's different when you feel slightly better. Just notice what's going on when the problems you have told me about today seem a little better. What's different that is making things a little better? Remember, we're not looking for times when the problem totally disappears, just times when it seems a little easier

Date/Time	What's been different? What were you doing? How did it make you feel?

The more differences you can bring back to the next session the sooner we can start finding solutions that will make a difference to you!

Exercise example: what is it you like to do?

Complete the table below. Try to think of as many activities as you can – anything you currently like to do, used to like doing and anything you would like to do in the future when you are feeling better and more confident. Let your imagination go wild. I promise I won't hold you to anything!

Activities I used to like doing	
Exercise biking	Working
Clubbing/dancing	Listening to new music
Drinking/pubbing	Playing board games
Going out for meals	Sex – is this classed as an activity?!
Having parties	Spending lots of time with my brother and sister
Badminton	Cooking for my mum
Kick boxing	

Activities I currently enjoy doing	
Walking	Netball
Reading (books for pleasure – not textbooks!)	Babysitting
Cinema	Bird watching (don't laugh!)

Activities I may like to try in the future	
Pilates/yoga	Voluntary work – home or abroad
Badminton	Arts and crafts related evening course
Meditation	

Exercise: what is it you like to do?

Complete the table below. Try to think of as many activities as you can – anything you currently like to do, used to like doing and anything you would like to do in the future when you are feeling better and more confident. Let your imagination go wild. I promise I won't hold you to anything!

Activities I used to like doing

Activities I currently enjoy doing

Activities I may like to try in the future

Exercise: problems versus resources

1 Take a blank piece of A4 paper.

2 Divide it into two halves by drawing a line down the middle.

3 On the left-hand side, write down a problem that is real and current – try to summarise it in 10 words or less.

4 On the right-hand side, write down your resources, your own and others' experience in solving problems, people that could help you with this problem or have helped you before, resources on the internet that could help – *anything!* Be creative!

5 Tear down the centre of the page.

6 Which of these two halves do you want to keep – the problem or resources?

Scrunch up into a ball and throw away the half you don't want.

'Life is not a problem to be solved but a reality to be experienced.'

Kierkegaard Quoted in Winokur (1989, p76)

(exercise inspired and adapted from a presentation by Steve Freeman, found on UK Association of Solution Focused Practitioners' website [www.ukasfp.co.uk]; original author unknown)

Of course, problems don't just disappear if we write them down and then throw them away. If SFT could do that for you, there would be no other types of therapies! But this exercise does do a couple of really useful things. The process of writing down in a limited number of words what our problem is allows us to focus on what is really causing us distress. Even when our lives are filled with many problems, being asked to highlight just one of them can lead to increased clarity of what the issue is. What was once a mountain of unsolvable problems becomes a single, more manageable issue for which we can start finding solutions.

With the problem conveniently tossed to one side, the client is left with the start of a solution – resources they have identified as something they could use in order to make the problem a little more manageable. By working with our clients to lengthen this list and then to actually get them to start using these resources, clients are empowered to tackle not only their current problem but a whole range of generic problems.

Occasionally, clients will scrunch up and throw out their resources, preferring instead to keep their problem. This helps us determine how much these individuals are committed to solution building. In these cases, we simply need to work on the client's motivation or further assess the client to determine if psychological therapy would be beneficial at this time.

Finding that positive lens

A common goal people seem to bring to therapy is to be happy. When people answer the Miracle Question, or tell me about their preferred future, they tell me that all they want to be is happy.

'The aspects of things that are most important for us are hidden because of their simplicity and familiarity.'

Wittgenstein Quoted in Winokur (1989, p133)

But how realistic is it – to be happy all the time? How many people do you know who are always happy? Happiness can be temporal – something or someone can make us happy, but the feeling usually doesn't last long. Personally I don't see the opposite of being depressed as being happy. What I encourage my clients to aim for is to be content and fulfilled with themselves. Simply put – I encourage them to aim for the middle ground of being OK. This is a more permanent state. And more importantly it can be directly influenced by what they do.

Good mental health and a positive sense of well-being are transient states and we need to do whatever we can to maintain them. We're surrounded by a barrage of messages telling us we're not OK. We only need to turn on the TV and within half an hour we would have received an onslaught of messages telling us we need to have this in our lives or that we need to be doing that. Then there is the news. If it's not the next pandemic threat, it's worries about the economy or our jobs. More threats to our sense of well-being.

I'm not trying to blame the media, but for most of us it's an inescapable part of life. Soap operas can give us the opposite message. We like watching them as they tell us we are OK compared to the people caught up in the current storyline.

Our friends and families can also erode our sense that we're OK. Some do it directly. Sometimes it's because of our ongoing ability to negatively compare ourselves to one or more of them, perhaps our best friend or elder sibling. The negative lens takes over and we see ourselves not how they might see us, but for everything we're not.

As we go through our day there is a whole host of stimuli that can either maintain our sense of well-being or damage it. Focusing on the 'If onlys …' and the 'What could have beens …' generally leads to a downward spiral of negative thinking. By training our clients to simply accept themselves and the things that they do and have done, their sense of well-being will be maintained. In effect, we want to help our clients make that permanent switch from a negative to a more positive lens.

Examples of an average day for me from a negative lens and from a positive lens	
Positive lens	**Negative lens**
Got up earlier than I had to in order to exercise.	Could have done more exercise but hit the snooze button.
Gave bathroom a quick clean so it looked OK.	Should have spent longer making the bathroom spotless.
Ate a very healthy breakfast.	Isn't healthy eating expected? I need to eat better all the time.
Compliment from my client. Client ready to move on as our work is coming to an end.	Client is moving on so need to worry about income.
Difficult session with client working on some tough issues – client left feeling OK.	Should really analyse the session so I can do better next time.
Managed to fit in a quick trip to the supermarket on way home.	Forgot a couple of items when I popped into the supermarket.

Don't get me wrong – I don't sit there thinking what a wonderful productive person I am. My self-talk simply focuses more on the positives, maintaining my sense of, 'Actually, I'm OK. My life is ticking over OK.' Negative thoughts and problems will always surface – no amount of solution focused work will eradicate that – but the more I use the positive lens in my self-talk, the more my self-efficacy will remain intact.

So ask your clients to shout about their achievements. Help them find that positive lens, the other side of the coin. And when they get lost, point them in the right direction. In time, by repeatedly doing this exercise, it becomes less of a task to search for the positives.

Even when the client has completed the exercise, it's your job to listen out for the positives the client may be missing. Each meeting with the client gives you a further opportunity to readjust the client's lens. Eventually the lens will become more of a permanent fixture.

When being 'OK' is not enough

Many clients are simply not happy with being OK. They don't want to see themselves as average. They argue with me that they want to aim higher, be better, the best. And who am I to take that away from them?

'Finding that positive lens' isn't about settling for being average or second best, it's simply about paying attention to all the evidence that you experience on a daily basis that could tell you that you're OK, not just the evidence that tells you that you're outstanding and exceptional.

Being 'OK' will probably mean something different for each person. Looking for the minimum evidence required to tell us that we're OK will allow for a continuation of good mental health.

Sometimes it can help to quantify the evidence. The examples above can generally be seen as being a 'C' grade. It's simple, everyday stuff that tells me I'm OK. For example, a small, simple message that tells me that I'm OK each day is that I made it into work. For me, this is just one of many positive self-complimenting statements that are filtered in through my positive lens. This is a 'C' grade message.

However, if I get consistent feedback from my clients that they find coming to our sessions useful, this would be 'B' grade evidence. And if my supervisor tells me that a piece of work I've done with a client is very creative, this is seen as an 'A' grade message. When my positive lens focuses on this evidence, that is, I've done more than expected of myself, my sense of achievement and sense of well-being increase.

Re-evaluating your expectations

If your clients always see themselves as needing 'A' grade evidence just to feel OK, they may have unrealistic expectations of themselves and be unable to maintain that grade all of the time. This can lead to them filtering out all the 'B' and 'C' grade evidence that tells them that they're OK.

As an example, consider someone who can only feel OK when they can achieve everything that is expected of them 100 per cent of the time. They need to complete all tasks set, have the perfect social life, perfect figure, perfect diet and the perfect life. Only when they see that they have achieved all this can they feel OK.

But what if they don't achieve it? Their positive lens is set so high that only 'A' grade evidence filters into their sense of being OK. All the other great stuff they do is missed, and they end up feeling disheartened, imperfect and a failure. By taking note of the 'B' and 'C' grade evidence, their confidence and esteem is sufficiently bolstered so they can continue to achieve the goals they want.

Work with your clients to elicit all the evidence from them that tells them they are OK.

Exercise: finding that positive lens

- Each day, try to focus on the messages you can give yourself that tell you that 'I'm OK'.
- Note down examples of what you've achieved each day, no matter how small.
- Start looking for messages that tell you 'I'm OK'.
- Initially this can be hard – for most of us our natural, default position of looking at what we do is very negative; we look for deficits in ourselves and our lives, focusing on the things we haven't achieved.
- When you find yourself stuck looking through a negative lens, simply ask yourself, 'How is looking at this situation in this negative way helpful to me?'
- Still stuck? Ask yourself how you would respond to a friend who only gave you negative aspects of their day. Treat yourself to the same compassion you would show your friend.

DAY:

Great escape

I've lost count of the number of times a client has stated mid-session that they wish they could just get away from it all, escape from their problems, leaving everything behind. And if we're honest, who hasn't felt that way at least once in their lives? Sometimes anywhere must be better than the place we find ourselves in at that moment of desperation.

But have we ever imagined what that great escape might look like? Or given any thought to what might happen when we get to where we want to be? The majority of us may not actually want to leave where we are – the 'great escape' being purely wishful thinking. But by exploring with our clients what their great escape may look like we can gain valuable insight into what's important to our clients and their preferred future. With this we can find yet more solutions, without actually having to escape. Let's look at an example:

'Twenty years from now you will be more disappointed by the things you didn't do than by the ones you did do. So throw off the bowlines, sail away from the safe harbour. Catch the trade winds in your sails. Explore. Dream. Discover.'

Mark Twain
(Quoted in Yamada, 2007)

Exercise example: great escape

Imagine you can actually escape from the confines of your problems. Start to plan this great escape ...

Where would you live?

Brighton – on the beach, by the sea.

What would you take?

Teddy bear, tent, duvet, books and a few photographs.

What would you leave behind?

Memories, stress, my flat, responsibility, sadness.

Who would you take?

Nobody (on a bad day). Everyone who I love (on a good day).

Why?

I want to be by myself (on a bad day). To have fun with friends (on a good day).

And who might you leave behind?

Family and friends (on a bad day). Ex-partners (on a good day).

List the things you'd have to take, the things that make you feel good about yourself.

I'm not a 'things person' – happy owning little. I wouldn't need to take anything apart from maybe make-up.

What would you like to be escaping to?

Peace, safety, calm, happiness, laughter, fun, open space/fresh air, freedom.

Exercise: great escape

Sometimes we all want to get away from everything and leave our problems behind. But what would it actually be like to put those plans into action?

Imagine you can actually escape from the confines of your problems. Start to plan this great escape ...

Where would you live?

What would you take?

What would you leave behind?

Who would you take? Why?

And who might you leave behind?

List the things you'd have to take, the things that make you feel good about yourself.

What would you like to be escaping to?

Becoming what you want

Most of the time clients have a pretty good idea about the person they would like to be. It can be pretty well hidden by their problems, but generally they have a vision of how they would like to see themselves. This vision is based on their previous experience, how they see others, and their own dreams and desires.

'The search for happiness is one of the chief sources of unhappiness.'

Eric Hoffer
Quoted in Winokur (1989, p101)

Sometimes the area of dysfunction can be specific to a certain part of their lives but at other times it can be a more generic issue of simply not coping. The example I have used here looks at a more generic issue and asks the client to envisage themselves as someone who is coping with life's difficulties. But the exercise can work just as well in more specific ways, such as encouraging the client to see themselves in certain roles – as a parent, a child, in a relationship, as an employee, or as someone achieving success.

This exercise is adapted from a paper by Switek (2001) and is in itself highly adaptable depending on the needs of the client. The exercise incorporates most of the key elements of Solution Focused Therapy – preferred future, exceptions, scaling and goal setting. Initially the client is asked to notice their resources and possibilities and not just their deficits. For many clients this can be a stumbling block – so enmeshed with their problems, the client can struggle to see any resources or solutions.

The questions are designed to challenge the client's perception of their life and functioning in certain areas. This can lead to a re-scripting of their narrative together with increased confidence in that particular area. By bringing the client's resources to the surface, future solution building can and will occur.

Me as someone coping with life's difficulties

In the example below, the 'me as someone coping with life's difficulties' is interchangeable dependent on what the client wants to work on. If the client's most pressing issue is to look at their role as a parent, the exercise simply changes to 'me as a dad'. If the current stressor is more work related, the exercise changes to 'me as an employee' and so on. After the example, a blank form is provided which allows you to insert whatever the client wants to work on.

Wherever possible, encourage the client to work on this initially by themselves. If they start to struggle, get them to ask friends or family, finishing off with them working directly with you as the practitioner.

A great way to get the client to start imagining themselves in a particular way is to ask them to think of a role model. This could be someone from their immediate life or someone fictional – clients pick from the magnitude of characters in film, TV and books. Once they have this role model, explore with them what it is about that person or character that they like. From there simply break down what they see into a set of skills that they can start to emulate.

Common answers

Generally this exercise induces answers that relate to a set of skills that the client feels they are lacking, such as confidence, assertiveness, anger management, and so on. By eliciting from the client how they view themselves we have broken down what was once an unmanageable problem into a problem with many solutions.

Skills deficits can be corrected by allowing the client to access appropriate services where they can learn such skills. In some cases, you as the practitioner can teach these skills. At a minimum, the client can be directed to self-help books where they can increase their skills base and feel more adept at becoming what they want.

Exercise example: becoming what you want

Think about what it means to you as someone who copes with life's difficulties. When you think about 'me as someone who copes with life's difficulties', let your imagination run wild and answer the following:

1 What are your best hopes when coping with life's difficulties? Give examples of how you see yourself coping with life's difficulties.

Calmly and rationally. In control of situation. Asking for help when available. Without 'losing it'.

2 Has there ever been a time when you have coped, even to a small degree, a little like you described above? Times when you could say, 'I coped with that really well'?

When my boyfriend finished with me – after the initial upset I was able to be quite calm and rational.

3 On the basis of the above examples and other ones you might have in mind, try to fill out the following table.

What have you learned over the course of your years that tells you about what you are capable of? What abilities have you developed? What kind of personality features can you show that are helpful in working effectively in a way that you like?

What was I able to do?	What abilities did I show in that situation?	What features of my personality did I show?
Come to terms with the end of the relationship and 'move on'.	*Looked to the future. Realised I was better off not being in the relationship.*	*I was mentally strong.*
Coped with being picked on at work.	*In the end I told my manager about it – confided in them. Stood up for myself.*	*I was confident. Trusted someone to help me.*

4 What was helpful and useful to you when coping with life's difficulties?
Try to identify what was useful inside of you (your own internal resources, skills and abilities) and outside of you (for example, other people, technology).

Inside you	Outside of you
Self-worth.	*Support from manager and friends.*
Inner strength – stood up for myself.	*Vodka!*
Self-confidence.	*Threw myself into work.*
Ability to relax.	

5 Please estimate your current level of coping with life's difficulties on a scale of zero to ten, where zero stands for 'I am not coping with life's difficulties' and ten stands for 'I am coping very well with life's difficulties'.

0	1	2	3	4	5	6	7	8	9	10
						X				

6 Tell me what you are doing, thinking or feeling, what others are doing, or what is going on for you, that puts you at the level you indicated in the previous question.

Getting on with life.
Not thinking about it too much.

7 What stops this figure being one point lower? What are you doing to stop this?

Meeting up with friends.
Trying to think positive.
Not going out and getting drunk.

8 What do you think you need to do next to move one point up the scale?

Start thinking about finding another relationship.
Get a better work–life balance.

Exercise: becoming what you want

Think about what it means to you as someone who copes with life's difficulties. When you think about 'me as someone who copes with life's difficulties', let your imagination run wild and answer the following:

1 What are your best hopes when coping with life's difficulties? Give examples of how you see yourself coping with life's difficulties.

2 Has there ever been a time when you have coped, even to a small degree, a little like you described above? Times when you could say, 'I coped with that really well'?

3 On the basis of the above examples and other ones you might have in mind, try to fill out the following table.

What was I able to do?	What abilities did I show in that situation?	What features of my personality did I show?

4 What was helpful and useful to you when coping with life's difficulties?
Try to identify what was useful inside of you (your own internal resources, skills and abilities) and outside of you (for example, other people, technology).

Inside you	Outside of you

5 Please estimate your current level of coping with life's difficulties on a scale of zero to ten, where zero stands for 'I am not coping with life's difficulties' and ten stands for 'I am coping very well with life's difficulties'.

0	1	2	3	4	5	6	7	8	9	10

6 Tell me what you are doing, thinking or feeling, what others are doing, or what is going on for you, that puts you at the level you indicated in the previous question.

7 What stops this figure being one point lower? What are you doing to stop this?

8 What do you think you need to do next to move one point up the scale?

My life as a movie

'Imagination is more important than knowledge.'

Albert Einstein
Quoted in Winokur (1989, p106)

No matter how many different ways you try to ask a client about where they see themselves in the future, what goals they would like to work on, or any future orientated plans, they can still struggle to see past their debilitating problems.

At times like this we need Hollywood to get involved. In a similar vain to the Miracle Question mentioned elsewhere in this book, 'My life as a movie' encourages clients to use their imagination to help them generate a preferred future, attainable goals, exceptions and real solutions. At other times it will simply strengthen the therapeutic relationship and give the client an inkling of hope for a better future.

This exercise encourages clients to see their life up until the present moment as a movie. Autobiographical in nature, this film is the story of how they have come to be up to this point in time. The therapist gets the client to be the director of this film, deciding the genre of the film (horror, comedy, thriller, etc), the leading actor or actress and who will play the supporting roles.

The tough part comes next. Working with the therapist, the client decides how they would like this movie to end – from now until a point of their choosing. This could be with the leading character's death or the achievement of their desire. The possibilities will be endless. More importantly, the possibilities will be individual, generated from your client.

This exercise validates what can be a difficult client history, allowing the client to go into whatever depths they need to with the therapist. From this problem-focused dialogue, the therapist encourages the client to recognise whatever resources they may have used to get them to the point where they are now and to a position of looking forward. No matter what struggles someone has been faced with, in a movie of their life they would want to make the most of their triumphs over adversity. From this we learn about client resources.

Exercise: my life as a movie

Autobiographical in nature, this film is the story of your life up to this point in time. You are the director of this film, deciding the genre of the film (horror, comedy, thriller, etc), the leading actor or actress and who will play the supporting roles.

Once you have thought about the main scenes to date, start thinking about how you would like to see the movie turn out from today. With this movie, tell me how you would like to write it from here – if it is going to be a full movie, would it have a good ending? How would you achieve this? For the movie, imagine the next steps you would need to take to achieve this ending you want. Who would play you? Where would it be set?

Struggling with writing the whole movie ...

While thinking about your life as a movie for a second, if you were to pause this movie on the best bit, what would it be? Why is that part so good? How come that bit in particular is so good?

Movies not your thing ...

Can't see yourself on the silver screen? How about in paperback?

Use the exercise but go about it as if you are writing your autobiography.

Start with a chapter plan – what chapters would you put in your book so far? What are the most memorable parts? Which parts of your life have defined you as a person? What is it about you that you would like the world to know?

End with the chapters you would like to include in the future. How would you like to see your life progress from here? What would the chapters look like? How do you see yourself in your final years? What achievements would you like to write about?

Exercise: my life as a movie

Title of movie:

Genre:

Director: (insert client's name)

Assistant Director: (insert therapist's name)

Cast: leading and supporting roles played by:

Main scenes to date:

Ending of the movie:

Best bit of the movie:

Major scenes from now until the end of the movie:

Living your life by the toss of a coin

Clients can at times come up with some wonderful solutions to their problems. With gentle encouragement, individuals are able to see what it is they need to do to instigate a small change to their situation in order to make their lives better. At other times, during our conversations with them, they can let slip an area of their lives that could be made better by simply doing something slightly different.

Once these small changes have been identified, clients can be reluctant to try something new because they fear they might fail or that they may continue to feel stuck. Clients with high levels of depression or anxiety can struggle to make the simplest decisions as to what course of action they should take. Allowing the toss of a coin to determine whether we should venture into unchartered, new behaviour, allows an external, inanimate object to decide on what we should do.

One of the most important aspects of this exercise is for the client to note down what was different about a day when the coin came up as 'heads' because this could lead into further solutions. It will also tell you as the practitioner whether the solution they are trying needs to be modified in any way.

This is a surprisingly simple but effective exercise. Although initially reluctant to fully engage with the exercise, clients often come back to me saying they wish it had been 'heads' more often as they felt they had better days when it was heads!

Example

Susan was very concerned about her weight, and as a result would weigh herself at every possible opportunity. The main problem seemed to be when she weighed herself at the start of the day. She told me that if her weight had gone down, she would have a good day, and if it had stayed the same or gone up her mood would go down and she would have a bad day. Despite educating Susan on the daily fluctuations in weight normal in the course of a day, she still continued to weigh herself. Susan was encouraged to use the coin toss exercise to see if her mood would be more stable independent of her weight.

Although she found not weighing herself hard, she managed to live her life by the toss of a coin, and after the first week found that her mood remained more stable if she didn't weigh herself in the mornings. Susan had removed an external force (the weighing scales) from determining how her day would be.

Exercise: living your life by the toss of a coin

Problem Area:
possible Solutions:

Each evening before you go to bed, toss a coin.

Next day, if it is heads, do the proposed alternative behaviour; the solution.

If it is tails, go about your day as usual.

At the end of a day when the coin has come up as heads, note down what has been *different* about that day.

No cheating. Repeated coin toss or best of three is not allowed!

If the coin is heads I will ...		
Day	Heads or tails	What was different about the day?
Monday		
Tuesday		
Wednesday		
Thursday		
Friday		
Saturday		
Sunday		

Is it in you? Qualities of a good person

Low self-worth seems to accompany a whole host of problems. When depression takes hold, the client can struggle to see anything positive about themselves. Constantly focusing on the negative aspects of themselves and their lives, the client struggles to see what value they can be to anyone.

'There is more in us than we know. If we can be made to see it, perhaps, for the rest of our lives, we will be unwilling to settle for anything less.'

Kurt Hahn (Quoted in Yamada, 2007)

In my experience, by completing this exercise clients learn to see themselves in a more objective way, and start to gather evidence with the practitioner that points to increased self-worth. It has proved invaluable with my work with survivors of sexual abuse who constantly state that they feel they have nothing to offer anyone. As the exercise is tailored to the client, they select the qualities they feel are relevant to them – this further increases the client's sense of self.

By asking other people in their social network about what characteristics make up a good person, the client learns to broaden their thinking, and on occasion this can be all that is necessary for them to start to see their own personalities in a different way.

As the list grows, I often encourage my clients to start living their lives 'as if' they have more of that quality for a specific week. This allows the client to see how their life could be better if they *do something* a little different that they know will make them feel better.

Exercise: Is it in you? Qualities of a good person

Complete the table below – start by filling in as many qualities of what you think makes a good person as you can. Ask as many people as possible for their opinions.

Starting with your first quality, in the second column write down what this quality means to you. *For example, if the first quality is Caring, to me this would mean ...*

Next, find a good dictionary and look up all the possible definitions of the word 'caring'. See if it matches or adds to how you defined it.

In the next column, write down how much between 1 and 100 you feel you have of that quality – how much is in you. *Continuing with our example of caring, if you feel you are quite a caring person, you could enter 70 in that box.*

In the next column, write down what you feel you would need to be doing to have 10 per cent more on your scale of this quality. *Returning to the example, to feel 80 on the scale this person would be calling her friends a couple of times a week.*

Each week research and think about a different quality. In between each week, try living your life 'As if' you had that higher score. What would you be doing? How would people around you notice that you had more of this quality in you? When would you know that you had 'enough' within you to feel more human again?

Qualities of a good person

Quality	Definition	Percentage you currently have (1–100)	What would be different if you had another 10 per cent?
Caring	*Concern for others. Protecting others; looking out for them; helpful.*	*70*	*Visit my mum more often. Offer to help my friend more.*

Turning the alphabet into solutions

The A–Z exercise can be effective as either a stand-alone exercise or as a springboard to finding solutions. As the client comes up with the words which describe them at their best, you as the practitioner can work with them to find exceptions – times when they felt they were what the word describes (or times when they were close to it). From these exceptions we can see if there is anything the client can re-create currently in order to ease their problem.

If the client feels that they have never really experienced being the words that describe them at their best, we can use some of these words as possible goals the client could work towards. For example:

Therapist: So one of the words you used to describe yourself at your best was assertive. What exactly does that mean to you?

Client: Ermm. I guess it's about making myself heard, about getting what I'm thinking and feeling across to other people.

Therapist: OK, good. Have there ever been times when you feel you have been assertive?

Client: No, not really. I always let others talk over me. It's hard for me to tell people how I'm feeling.

Therapist: But it seems it's something you want to be. How would it feel to make being more assertive a goal you could work towards?

As can be seen, the therapist starts off by determining what the client means by the words listed. Although this may seem a pretty mundane task, it ensures that both client and therapist are on the same page, putting the client well and truly in the role as expert and allowing the therapist to use the words and meaning generated by the client.

Clients tend to really enjoy this exercise. It is a very gentle way of finding exceptions and generating small goals the client can work on. When used in group situations, clients realise that some of the words generated by others may apply to them or are words they would like to apply to them, giving you as a practitioner the opportunity to develop more solutions.

Exercise example: the A–Z of me at my best

This is a fun and relatively simple exercise to ask clients to do. It is a work in progress exercise – it can be hard to do in one go but it is great to add to as your work with the client progresses. It's easily adaptable to groups as a brainstorming exercise, and can work with both clients and trainees.

All the exercise entails is for the client to write down words that describe them when they are at their best, or how they would like to describe themselves at their best. As words come to mind, they simply add them to the list if they apply. Over time they produce a list of positive words about themselves – great to add to the 'Solutions scrapbook' discussed later in this section.

The A–Z of me!			
A	Affordable, Assertive, Ace	**N**	Nice, Naughty, Novel
B	Broad, Brave, Bold	**O**	Optimistic, Ordinary
C	Compassionate, Caring, Confident	**P**	Passionate, Punctual, Positive
D	Direct, Delightful, Drop Dead Gorgeous	**Q**	Quirky
E	Engaging, Enthusiastic, Encouraging	**R**	Rational, Radiant, Reliable, Randy, Realistic
F	Funny, Friendly, Forward	**S**	Special, Singular, Systematic, Sweet, Sexy
G	Gorgeous, Generous	**T**	Tenacious, Tender, Therapeutic
H	Hospitable, Huggable, Happy	**U**	Underrated, Understanding, Unique
I	Intelligent, Interesting, Intriguing	**V**	Vivacious, Vivid
J	Jolly, Joker	**W**	Wonderful, Weird, Warm, Welcoming, Willing
K	Kind, Knowledgeable, Kinky	**X**	Xtra-ordinary, X-treme
L	Loveable, Loyal, Likeable	**Y**	Youthful, Young, Young at heart
M	Motherly, Modest	**Z**	Zealous, Zany

Exercise: the A–Z of me at my best

Write down the words that describe you at your best, or how you would like to describe yourself at your best.

The A–Z of me!			
A		N	
B		O	
C		P	
D		Q	
E		R	
F		S	
G		T	
H		U	
I		V	
J		W	
K		X	
L		Y	
M		Z	

Building your perfect world

This exercise is designed to really allow your client's imagination to start working. Its inspiration came from a song called 'World' by an American band called Five For Fighting. The song describes the arrival of a package, and on the side of the box is printed 'A.C.M.E.'s Build-a-World-to-be'. The recipient is allowed to build the type of world they would want to live in.

'What kind of world do you want? Think Anything
Let's start at the start, Build a masterpiece
Be careful what you wish for, History starts now ...

Should there be people or peoples, Money, Funny pedestals for Fools who never pay
Raise your Army – Choose your Steeple, Don't be shy, the satellites can look the other way

Lose the Earthquakes – Keep the Faults, Fill the oceans without the salt.'

Ondrasik (2006)

Many clients come to us wanting a better world. Many of their problems seem out of their control – they see their problems as bigger, world issues, which on the surface they are powerless to do anything about. And some of the problems are bigger than them. No amount of counselling will make the sun shine more often or make automated telephone systems a thing of the past.

By focusing on these global issues the client becomes a victim. They see the problem as being out of their control, and become paralysed by the enormity of the situation. They learn to be helpless, and in the process they ignore the smaller skills and resources they could be using to make their situation a little better.

Encourage them to start big – as the song lyrics above say, maybe fill the oceans without salt. And as they begin to see their world taking shape, gradually get them to think about their immediate world, and how they would like this to be.

And then, as with the other exercises focused on helping the client describe their preferred future, discover what the client would be *doing* differently if this world was a reality. When you've exhausted what they would be doing, thinking and feeling, see if they could try to do any of those things, or whether there are any times when part of the actions and thoughts they describe are already happening. Could they live 'as if' their world is a reality for a day just to see how their lives may be different?

If you can get the client to really engage with you in this exercise, the results can reveal some great solutions. Imagining their perfect world can temporarily remove them from the confines of their problems. Once engaged in a different way of thinking, clients will always surprise you with the solutions they find.

Exercise: building your perfect world

Imagine for a moment that you've been given the task to design a whole new world. Your world.

Everything that frustrates you and depresses you about the current world can be eliminated. Anything you struggle with can be eradicated.

What would your world look like? Allow your imagination to run wild – would the sun shine all the time? Would money grow on trees? Would you be able to have relationships without any hurt? Would chocolate be good for you?

Once you've found the solution to world issues, what would your immediate world look like?

If these changes were to happen, what might be different for you? What would you be doing? How would you be feeling? What type of things would you be thinking?

Is there any part of this that is already happening now?

The solution is confidence

Regardless of the type of presenting problem, a lack of confidence always seems to be lurking around in the background, either caused directly by the problem or as a problem in itself. I've lost count of the number of times clients come for help wanting to increase their confidence.

'I was always looking outside myself for strength and confidence but it comes from within. It is there all the time.'
Anna Freud (Quoted by Thinkexist.com)

When working with clients to increase their confidence, it is important to encourage them to define exactly what confidence means to them; how would they define confidence? Over time, I've come to see self-confidence as a belief in yourself and your abilities; as freedom from doubt; as a belief in your ability and value; as having trust in people, plans and the future; and as having respect for oneself and one's worth as a person.

Clients often have a number of myths about self-confidence that need to be explored. Before you can start helping them re-discover their confidence, it can be useful to explore their myths. Three common ones are explored below.

Box 8.2 Common myths about self-confidence

You have to be born with it.

Self-confidence is a set of skills that can be learned, just like learning to drive or playing a game.

If you've had your confidence destroyed, it's gone forever.

It may take a great leap of faith to start building it back up, but once you're there you'll be much stronger than you were before and less likely to have your confidence shaken again.

I know I'm confident when I can be sure I'll succeed at something new.

How can you know you'll succeed when you've never done something before? Confidence is more about tolerating uncertainty and about coping when things don't go as planned. It's about trying new things to start rebuilding confidence.

Self-confidence is an essential part of feeling good. It makes us feel proud of ourselves and what we can do. Self-confidence gives us the courage to try new things and the power to believe in ourselves. It sometimes is the solution but nearly always facilitates solutions to happen.

Exercise: confidence and you

This exercise encourages you to assess the areas where you already have confidence and areas where you want confidence. When you have been able to identify an area where you already have confidence, think about what it is about that area that gives you confidence. Explore if any part of these skills can be transferred to an area where you don't feel quite as confident.

Note down and identify situations where you already have confidence.

What abilities do you have confidence in?

List the situations where you want to be more confident.

Things you will be able to do once you have this confidence.

Start small. Most people have confidence in brushing their teeth or in crossing the road. These can be the starting point in helping you to identify that you do have some confidence. When the hard work of identifying existing confidence is done, use the second two lists as possible goals you may want to work on, breaking them down into achievable, manageable steps.

Exercise: your model of confidence

There's nothing original about confidence. We're not trying to re-invent the wheel. Sometimes having a person we can copy can be a start to the confidence solution. This exercise encourages you to do just that – to think of a role model when it comes to confidence and start thinking whether you can replicate what makes them confident.

Think of a person who you consider to be self-confident in a situation where you would like to be confident.

Write down what it is that lets you know that that person is confident – make it specific. For example, rather than, 'the way he looks', write 'his face is relaxed and smiling a little'.

Cover all aspects of the person: facial expression, posture, voice tone (loud, soft, deep), gestures, the way they dress, how they interact with others, how others react to them.

Anything else you notice about them.

Reasons to feel good: doing that solution in detail

Clients can give you endless reasons why they have failed. But with the right coaching they can do the same for what went right. Cognitive Behaviour Therapy (CBT) tells us that by challenging our problematic, negative automatic thoughts we can re-learn a more rational way of thinking, which in turn will affect the way we feel and the way we behave. Thought records have become standard operating procedure with the majority of CBT practitioners. By and large they are successful at helping individuals modify their thoughts and manage their anxiety and depression.

Currently CBT only looks at the negative thoughts; the times when we perceive events that happen in our lives as negative. CBT helps us to re-align our thoughts to help us overcome our problems. The exercise 'Doing that solution in detail' reverses this problem-focused slant on our thoughts and helps us to pinpoint what worked and why. It helps us to expand on events and the associated thoughts and beliefs about them, but more importantly looks at how we can replicate some or all of how we created that solution.

Initially clients may struggle – this is a new way of looking at the positive events in their lives. There may also be some resistance – clients may not see the point of analysing something that was good.

Others will simply put it down to 'good luck'. Those same clients, however, are reluctant to simply allow their failure to be down to 'bad luck'. Encourage clients away from seeing the world as a series of good-and-bad luck events; by analysing the positives in their lives, they can start to regain some control over their lives, and start creating more solutions.

Exercise: reasons to feel good: doing that solution in detail

- As the client begins to recognise more positive events in their lives, encourage them to fill in the following thought record which encourages them to really dissect what was good about an event and why.
- This exercise uses the scaling technique. Even for those really positive events, most people usually analyse how it could have been even better.
- By analysing how confident the client is that they can replicate part of the solution, the client can start to develop resources to ensure that parts of it happen again
- Completed thought records should be placed in the Solutions scrapbook.

Exercise example: reasons to feel good: doing that solution in detail

Event	I got the job!
Positive thoughts and beliefs	1 I'm a success. 2 I know what I'm talking about. 3 I'm a good person.
Feelings	Pride. Relaxed. Happy. Content. Relief.
Evidence to support the thoughts and beliefs	1 Over 10 people were interviewed and they chose me. 2 When I put my mind to something sometimes I surprise myself at what I can achieve. 3 Previous employers have always spoken highly of me and now I feel I'm starting to believe them.
Resources used	Prepared for the interview – researched the company, wrote down my experience and how it related to the position I was being interviewed for. Practised interview techniques. Used my relaxation skills to remain calm during the interview.
Action needed to replicate this solution	Preparation. Relaxation techniques. Confidence in self and abilities in order to put best self forward. Continuing enhancement of skills.
Confidence that you can use parts of this solution again – zero to ten	Eight.
What you need to do to increase your confidence by one	More mock interviews.

Exercise: reasons to feel good: doing that solution in detail

Event	
Positive thoughts and beliefs	1 2 3
Feelings	
Evidence to support the thoughts and beliefs	1 2 3
Resources used	
Action needed to replicate this solution	
Confidence that you can use parts of this solution again – zero to ten	
What you need to do to increase your confidence by one	

Relationship shopping

This exercise works well for those either looking for a partner or for those who are simply not fulfilled in their current relationship. Giving clients the permission to fantasise about their perfect relationship is a starting point from which to work with that individual to find out what it is they want from a relationship.

The exercise gets clients to think about exactly what it is they want in a relationship, what they may be prepared to compromise on and what they need to do in order to find a match to their requirements. As well as encouraging them to fantasise about their ideal relationship, it also encourages them to focus their expectations on what might be more realistic.

Relationship problems are a common focus for a lot of our work. Even if relationships haven't been the initial presenting problem, scratch the surface and sure enough relationships will pop up.

Exercise: relationship shopping

- Imagine your local supermarket has a new aisle called 'Relationships'.
- In that aisle they have all the ingredients for the perfect relationship. Some things this aisle might contain could be good looks, compassion, respect, sense of humour, David Bekham, good hygiene and Cheryl Cole.
- Imagine you are in this supermarket and can have whatever you want from this aisle.
- What would your shopping basket (or if you really want, your shopping trolley) look like?
- When you've finished shopping, make two lists out of what you have in your basket; those items you need at all costs, and those that you may be willing to compromise on.
- Finally, make a list of what you might need to do differently in your life to try to find somebody who matches some or all of the items in your basket.

Points to remember

- Before you can start looking for a relationship you need to consider what it is you want in another person and from a relationship.
- If you go food shopping when you're really hungry, what do you end up buying? Probably loads of stuff you wouldn't normally buy but because you're really hungry you've put it in your basket as an 'impulse' buy. Relationship shopping can be similar – when you're 'hungry' for a relationship you may end up settling for someone you may otherwise not normally pick.

Solutions scrapbook

> **'When you seek it, you cannot find it.'**
>
> *Zen saying*

Solution Focused Therapy is all about building up our clients' resources so they can learn to identify solutions in problematic situations, both in their current situation and in the future.

Personally my memory isn't quite what it was, and at times I struggle to remember how I found a solution to something. My declining number of brain cells together with a tendency to remember more negative things than positive, can lend itself to me racking my brain to think of the solution I used the last time I was faced with a problematic situation (using this software package, for example!). Although I'm yet to come up with a solution to stop the ageing process (and let's face it, if I had I probably wouldn't be writing this book!), I've found using a solutions scrapbook to be the next best thing.

When clients start to experience even a modicum of success, encourage them to make up a scrapbook of what they did, why it worked and how it made them feel. I'm a realist, and know that as hard as we try to keep our lives on an even keel, something tends to come along to knock us off course. Sometimes the thing that knocks us off course is a wonderful, positive event, but unless we capture it, put it in our scrapbook, we run the risk of forgetting exactly what it was and how it made us feel. More importantly, we lose how we might use a small part of it against future tough times.

The solutions scrapbook exercise works for just about everybody. As a practitioner, you can choose your level of involvement from simply offering verbal encouragement to bringing in examples of solutions you have found that clients could incorporate into their scrapbook. It can be a fantastic visual explosion, or just a notebook with examples of what works and why. To aid the process, try using the 'Solution scavenger hunt' exercise from Chapter 5.

Why this works

By getting involved in collating as much evidence of solutions as possible, both from their behaviour and the world around them, clients not only build up their own resources but also start looking at their world from a more solution focused perspective.

For those clients who experience recurrent depression, having a tangible collection of solutions they have created in the past can at the very least halt the slide into a deeper depression. The solutions scrapbook can be something family, friends and professionals can draw on to support the individual.

What the solutions scrapbook becomes is a unique collection of times when the problem wasn't as bad. They become the exceptions.

References

References

American Heritage Dictionary of the English Language, The (2009) 4th edn, online, http://dictionary.reference.com/browse/compliment (accessed 15 August 2009).

Aristotle (384 BC–322 BC) online, www.thinkexist.com/quotations/anger/3.html (accessed 18 October 2009).

Aronson J (2009) Personal email communication, 6 October 2009.

Assay TP and Lambert MJ (1999) 'The empirical case for the common factors in therapy: quantitative findings', Hubble MA, Duncan BL and Miller S (eds) *The Heart and Soul of Change: What Works in Therapy*, American Psychological Association, Washington DC.

Bannink FP (2007) 'Solution focused brief therapy', *Journal of Contemporary Psychotherapy*, 37, pp87–94.

Berg IK (2009) SFTBA website, online, www.sftba.org (accessed 17 July 2009).

Berg IK and Miller SD (1992) *Working With the Problem Drinker: A Solution Focused Approach*, Norton, New York.

Berg IK and Reuss NH (1998) *Solutions Step by Step: A Substance Abuse Treatment Manual*, W.W. Norton & Co, London and New York.

Biddle S, Fox K and Boutcher S (2000) (eds) *Physical Activity and Psychological Wellbeing*, Routledge, London.

Breswick K (2009) Application for an Evidence-based Practice Review, online, www.oregon.gov/DHS/mentalhealth/ebp/ap/solution-focus.pdf (accessed 4 October 2009).

Carey TA, Carey M, Stalker K, Mullan RJ, Murray LK and Spratt MB (2007) 'Psychological change from the inside looking out: a qualitative investigation', *Counselling and Psychotherapy Research*, 7 (3), pp178–87.

Corey G (2005) *Theory and Practice of Counseling and Psychotherapy*, 7th edn, Brooks Cole, California.

Coyhis D (2000) 'Culturally specific addiction recovery for Native Americans', Krestan J (ed), *Bridges to Recovery*, The Free Press, New York.`

Dahl R, Bathel D and Carreon C (2000) 'The use of Solution Focused Therapy with an elderly population', *Journal of Systemic Therapies*, 19 (4), pp45–55.

e Castro S and Guterman J (2008) 'Solution Focused Therapy for families coping with suicide', *Journal of Marital and Family Therapy*, 34 (1), pp93–106.

de Jong P and Berg IK (2002) *Interviewing for Solutions*, Brooks/Cole Thomson Learning, California.

de Shazer S (1985) *Keys to Solutions in Brief Therapy*, Norton, New York.

de Shazer S and Dolan Y (2007) *More than Miracles*, The Haworth Press, USA.

www.dictionary.com (2009)

Eakes G, Walsh S, Markowski M, Cain H and Swanson M (1997) 'Family centred brief Solution-Focused Therapy with chronic schizophrenia: a pilot study', *Journal of Family Therapy*, 19, pp145–58.

Ferraz H and Wellman N (2009) 'Fostering a culture of engagement: an evaluation of a 2-day training in solution-focused brief therapy for mental health workers', *Journal of Psychiatric and Mental Health Nursing*, 16, pp326–34.

Fiske H and Zalter B (2005) 'Solution focused scavenger hunt', Nelson TS (ed), *Education and Training in Solution Focused Brief Therapy*, The Haworth Press Inc., USA.

Franklin C, Moore K and Hopson L (2008) 'Effectiveness of solution-focused brief therapy in a school setting', *Children and Schools*, 30 (1), pp15–26.

Gilliland BE and James RK (1993) *Crisis Intervention Strategies*, 2nd edn, Brooks/Cole, California.

Gingerich WA and Eisengart S (2000) 'Solution focused brief therapy: a review of the outcome research', *Family Process*, 39 (4), pp477–98.

Hall J and Marzillier J (2009) 'Alternative ways of working', *Psychologist*, 22 (5), pp406–7.

Haugh S and Paul S (2008) 'Is the relationship the therapy?' *Therapy Today*, 19 (10), pp34–7.

Hogg V and Wheeler J (2004) 'Miracles r them: solution focused practice in a social service duty team', *Practice*, 16 (4), pp299–314.

Hosany Z, Wellman N and Lowe T (2007) 'Fostering a culture of engagement: a pilot study of the outcomes of training mental health nurses working in two acute admission units in brief solution-focused therapy techniques', *Journal of Psychiatric and Mental Health Nursing*, 14, pp688–95.

Iveson C (2002) 'Solution focused brief therapy', *Advances in Psychiatric Treatment*, 8, pp149–56.

James W (1920) 'Letter to W. Lutoslawski 6th May 1906', *The Letters of William James (vol. 2)*. Atlantic Monthly Press, Boston, MA.

Kübler-Ross E (1969) *On Death and Dying*, Macmillan, New York.

LaFountain RM and Garner NE (1996) 'Solution focused counselling groups: the results are in', *Journal for Specialists in Group Work*, 21 (2), pp128–43.

Lambert MJ (1992) 'Implications of outcome research for psychotherapy integration', Norcross JC and Goldstein MR (eds), *Handbook of Psychotherapy Integration*, Basic Books, New York.

Lambert MJ, Okiishi JC, Finch AE and Johnson LD (1998) 'Outcome assessment: from conceptualization to implementation', *Professional Psychology: Research and Practice*, 29, pp63–70.

Lamprechet H, Laydon C, Mcquillan C, Wiseman S, Williams L, Gash A and Reily J (2007) 'Single-session solution-focused brief therapy and self-harm: a pilot study', *Journal of Psychiatric and Mental Health Nursing*, 14, pp601–2.

Lazarus AA (1996) 'The utility and futility of combining treatments in psychotherapy', *Clinical Psychology: Science and Practice*, 3 (1), pp59–68.

Macdonald A (2007) *Solution-Focused Therapy: Theory Research and Practice*, Sage, England.

Macdonald A (2010) Solution-Focused Therapy Brief Evaluation List, online, www.solutionsdoc.co.uk/sfb.html (accessed 11 September 2010).

McKergow MW and Korman H (2009) 'Inbetween – neither inside nor outside: the radical simplicity of Solution Focused Therapy', *Journal of Systemic Therapies*, 28 (2), pp34–49, online, http://www.sfwork.com/jsp/index.jsp?lnk=6d8 (accessed 12 September 2010).

Miller SD and Duncan B (2009) online, www.talkingcure.com (accessed 14 October 2009).

Murray CE and Murray TL (2004) 'Solution-focused premarital counseling: helping couples build a vision for their marriage', *Journal of Marital and Family Therapy*, 30 (3), pp349–58.

National Institute of Clinical Excellence, CG23 Depression, NICE Guidelines, online, http://guidance.nice.org.uk/CG90 (accessed 10 October 2009).

Neukrug ES and Schwitzer AM (2006) *Skills and Tools for Today's Counsellors and Psychotherapists*, Thomson Brooks Cole, California.

Ondrasik J (2006) 'World', *Two Lights by Five for Fighting*, EMI Blackwood Music Inc / Five for Fighting Music (BMI).

Piercy FP, Lipchik E and Kiser D (2000) 'Miller and De Shazer's article on "emotions in solution-focused therapy"', *Family Process*, 39, pp25–8.

Polich MJ, Armor DJ and Braiker HB (1980) *The Course of Alchoholism: Four Years after Treatment*, Rand Corporation, Santa Monica, CA.

Prochaska JO and DiClemente CC (1982) 'Transtheorectical therapy: toward a more integrative change', *Psychotherapy: Theory, Research and Practice*, 19, pp276–88.

Prochaska JO and Norcross JC (2001) 'Stages of change', *Psychotherapy*, 38, pp443–8.

Proudlock S (2009) 'Reflections on ... the assessment letter', *Healthcare Counselling and Psychotherapy Journal*, 9 (2), pp30–2.

Proudlock S and Hallé L (2006) 'Tapestry: a social relationships agency', *A Life in the Day*, 10 (1), pp15–17.

Reimer WL and Chatwin A (2006) 'Effectiveness of Solution Focused Therapy for affective and relationship problems in a private practice context', *Journal of Systemic Therapies*, 25 (1), pp52–67.

Rogers C (1951) *Client-centered Therapy: Its Current Practice, Implications and Theory*, Constable, London.

Sharry J (2007) *Solution-Focused Groupwork*, 2nd edn, Sage, London.

Sharry J, Darmody M and Madden B (2002) 'A solution-focused approach to working with clients who are suicidal', *British Journal of Guidance & Counselling*, 30 (4), pp383–99.

Shinn G (n.d.) Great-Quotes.com, online, *www.great-quotes.com* (accessed 24 December 2010)

Smith-Pickard P (2009) 'Sexuality in supervision', *Therapy Today*, 20 (2), pp28–31.

Solution Focused Brief Therapy Association, online, http://www.sfbta.org/research.html (accessed 4 October 2009).

Stams GJ, Dekovic M, Buist K and de Vries L (2006) 'Effectiviteit van oplossingsgerichte korte therapie; een meta-analyse [Efficacy of solution-focused brief therapy: a meta-analysis]', *Gedragstherapie [Behaviour Therapy]*, 39 (2), pp81–94.

Stevenson C, Jackson S and Barker P (2003) 'Finding solutions through empowerment: a preliminary study of a solution-oriented approach to nursing in acute psychiatric settings', *Journal of Psychiatric and Mental Health Nursing*, 10, pp688–96.

Strong T and Nielsen K (2008) 'Constructive conversations: revisiting selected developments with clients and counsellors', *Counselling and Psychotherapy Research*, 8 (4), pp253–60.

Switek T (2001) 'Deck of trumps – One of the ways for being helpful to clients and professionals in becoming what they want' (Polish Solutions Focused Team), Nelson TS (ed), *Education and Training in Solution Focused Brief Therapy*, The Haworth Press, Inc., USA.

Trepper TS, Dolan Y and McCollum EE (2006) 'Steve de Shazer and the future of solution focused therapy', *Journal of Marital and Family Therapy*, 32, pp133–9.

Trepper TS, McCollum EE, De Jong P, Korman H, Gingerich W and Franklin C (2010) 'Solution Focused Therapy treatment manual for working with individuals', *Research Committee of the Solution Focused Brief Therapy Association*, online, www.sfbta.org (accessed 17 September 2010).

Twain M (1836–1910) online, www.thinkexist.com/quotations/anger (accessed 18 October 2009).

UK Association for Solution Focused Practice Personal email communication. (2 February 2009)

Wampold BE (2001) *The Great Psychotherapy Debate*, Lawrence Erlbaum, New Jersey.
Webster DC, Vaughn K and Martinez R (1994) 'Introducing solution-focused approaches

to staff in inpatient psychiatric setting', *Archives of Psychiatric Nursing*, 8, pp254–61.

Wetchler JL (1990) 'Solution focused supervision', *Family Therapy*, XVII (2), pp129–38.

Wheeler J (2005) 'Solution focused training for social workers', Nelson TS (ed), *Education and Training in Solution Focused Brief Therapy*, The Haworth Press, Inc., USA.

Winokur J (1989) *Zen To Go*, Plume Book/Penguin, USA.

Yamada K (2005) *Live Good*, Compendium, Seattle, WA.

For Product Safety Concerns and Information please contact our EU representative GPSR@taylorandfrancis.com Taylor & Francis Verlag GmbH, Kaufingerstraße 24, 80331 München, Germany

Printed and bound by CPI Group (UK) Ltd, Croydon, CR0 4YY
14/09/2026
02216251-0003